From Your Friends at The MAILBOX®

730 Journal Prompts

Two for Every Day of the Year

Grades 4-6

W9-BEH-301

Editors:
Thad H. McLaurin and Cindy Mondello

Writers:
Marcia Barton, Karen Brudnak, Therese Durhman, Rusty Fischer,
Cindy Mondello, Patricia Twohey, David Webb

Art Coordinator:
Nick Greenwood

Artists:
Cathy Spangler Bruce, Teresa R. Davidson, Nick Greenwood,
Clevell Harris, Sheila Krill, Theresa Lewis, Rob Mayworth,
Kimberly Richard, Rebecca Saunders, Barry Slate

Cover Artist:
Nick Greenwood

www.themailbox.com

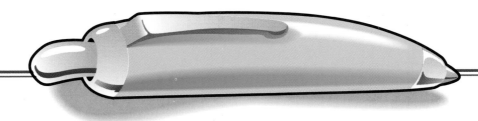

©1999 by THE EDUCATION CENTER, INC.
All rights reserved.
ISBN10 #1-56234-326-2 • ISBN13 #978-156234-326-2

Manufactured in the United States
10 9 8 7

Table of Contents

About This Book

This collection of over 730 journal prompts provides two journal prompts for every day of the year. The prompts are based on holiday, seasonal, and general topics, so an appropriate selection is always available to match your students' needs.

Reproducible journal covers and a lined writing page reproducible are also included, so solutions to all of your journal-writing needs are compiled in this handy resource.

How to Use This Book

Monthly Journal Response Booklets

Have each student create her own monthly journal response booklet. At the beginning of each month, make one copy of the appropriate monthly cover (see pages 100–111) for each student. Then make several copies of the lined writing page reproducible (see page 112) for each student. Stack the lined sheets of paper, place the monthly cover on top, and then staple along the left-hand side to create the booklet. Have each student decorate her cover with markers or crayons.

Guided Daily Journal Writing

Begin each day with an original, fun, thought-provoking journal prompt. Select one of the two prompts to write on the chalkboard, or write both prompts on the board and instruct each student to select the one that interests her the most. If you have access to an overhead projector, a transparency of the prompts will be a timesaver and can be reused year after year. Have students write their journal entries in their monthly journal response booklets. If desired, hold a class discussion of the daily writing topic before students begin writing.

Independent Journal Writing

Add an independent element to your journal-writing program with this idea. Post copies of a month's worth of journal prompts in a center, or display them in a prominent place in your classroom. Every day, challenge each child to select one prompt from the appropriate day to respond to in her monthly journal response booklet.

AUGUST

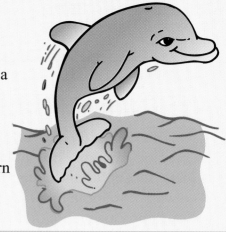

August 1

 Today is the birthday of Herman Melville, author of *Moby Dick*. Pretend you are a whale in the ocean being chased by a whaling ship. Describe what it is like to successfully avoid being harpooned and captured.

 You are sailing on the ocean and you notice a school of dolphins swimming alongside your yacht. Suddenly they turn and leave. You decide to follow. Where are they going? Describe what you see as you try to keep up with the dolphins.

August 2

 International Clown Week is held the first week in August. How do you think teachers feel when kids "clown around"? When is it appropriate to clown around? When is it inappropriate?

 Pretend you have just ordered the king-size, two-gallon ice-cream dessert at a local restaurant. The reward for finishing the ice-cream dish by yourself is that it's free! Describe how you manage to finish off the humongous dessert and the reaction of the crowd watching you.

August 3

 It's a hot August afternoon and there is a long line at your successful lemonade stand. An expensive-looking car pulls up, and the driver gets out and steps in front of everyone else in line. He then offers you $100 for the rest of your lemonade. Explain what you'd do and how the thirsty crowd waiting reacts to your decision.

 You're relaxing in your swimming pool on a quiet summer day when all of a sudden a parachutist lands in your backyard only a few feet away! What will you do? Who is this person, and why has he landed in your yard?

August 4

 You are cutting your uncle's lawn when suddenly his riding mower goes out of control, taking you down the street and onto the highway. Tell what happens next.

What's the most embarrassing thing that has ever happened to you when you were on vacation? Describe what happened and how you handled the situation.

August 5

Your parents have decided to build you your own apartment attached to the family home. What will you do on your first day in your new living quarters? Whom will you invite over as your first visitor?

Many kids your age have summer jobs such as mowing lawns, baby-sitting, delivering newspapers, and walking pets. If you could have any summertime job, what would it be and why?

August 6

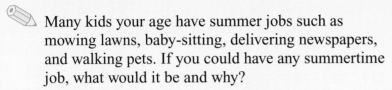

Imagine you're walking along a secluded beach with a metal detector looking for lost coins. Suddenly the detector starts to make a lot of noise, and your dog starts to bark furiously. What did you find?

As conductor of the community orchestra, you raise your hands and wave your baton to begin directing the musicians. Much to your surprise, the entire orchestra disappears! Could you have picked up a magic wand by accident? Describe what happens next and the audience's reaction.

August 7

On your first day as a lifeguard there is an exciting rescue and you are part of it! Tell what happens and why everyone is now calling you a hero.

Have you ever camped out in your backyard with a friend? Describe a time that you did camp out, or plan what you'd do if you were to have a campout with a friend this weekend.

August 8

If you could own a sea creature as a pet, what would it be? An octopus? A shark? Describe an adventure you might have with your unusual pet.

Do you have a nickname? Explain how you got this nickname and whether or not you like it. If you don't have a nickname, pick one for yourself and explain why you like it.

A U G U S T

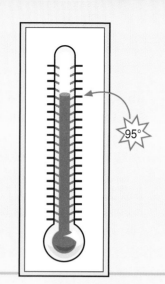

August 9

Write a short review about a book you've recently read. Also, if you were the author, explain whether or not you would have ended the book in a different way. If so, explain why and how you'd change the ending.

What's your favorite way to beat the heat? Is it taking a dip in a lake or a pool? How about eating ice cream or drinking ice-cold lemonade? Pretend it's 95°F outside and explain how you and a friend plan on staying cool.

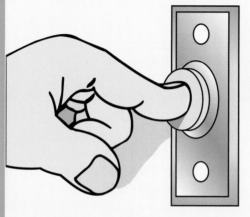

August 10

It is seven o'clock on a Saturday morning. The doorbell rings. You get out of bed and open the door. It is your best friend, who immediately tags you and says, "You're it!" before running away with several of your other friends. Describe what happens next.

What would be the perfect summer day for you? What kind of weather would it be? Where would you spend your day?

August 11

Often referred to as the longest word in the English language, pneumonoultramicroscopicsilicovolcanoconiosis is a disease of the lungs. Create your own word that is just as long (or longer) and give it a meaning. Then write a letter to the *Guinness Book of World Records* asking them to consider your word as a new record.

Smith, Jones, and *Brown* are very common American last names. What would it be like if these were the only surnames that people could have? Write a short essay explaining why you think it's important to have more than just three surnames.

SMITH FAMILY REUNION

August 12

Imagine that your parents don't know what lightning is and are frightened every time they see it. Write what you would say to them if you had to sit them down and explain it.

You are sitting on the edge of your pool when a glass soda bottle floats to the surface. You reach for the mysterious bottle and find a note inside. Write what the note says; then describe what you do next.

August 13

 Imagine that you are lying on your beach towel after swimming in the ocean. As you soak up the warm sun rays, you feel something poking your back beneath the towel. Describe what might be trying to poke its way out of the sand.

 Who is your favorite sports player? Describe what it is about this player that makes him/her your favorite. If you could be a member of this player's team, what position would you play?

DOOHICKEYS, GADGETS, AND THINGAMAJIGS FOR SALE

August 14

 Summer is often a time for family reunions. Write about your favorite relatives and what makes them so special. Then describe an activity your family might do at a reunion.

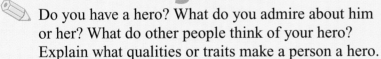 While on vacation in another state, your family drives past a roadside stand that has a sign reading "*Doohickeys, Gadgets,* and *Thingamajigs* for Sale." Your mom pulls the car over to check it out. Describe some of the items you find for sale, especially the one that your mom buys that's so big it has to be tied to the roof of the car!

August 15

 Do you have a hero? What do you admire about him or her? What do other people think of your hero? Explain what qualities or traits make a person a hero.

 Your mother wakes you up in the morning and says, "Guess what! We're going on vacation to Hawaii. Right now!" Tell how you'd react to this surprise and what you'd like to do when you land in the Aloha State.

HAWAII OR BUST!

August 16

 Imagine that you are fishing at a lake in the forest. You cast your line and suddenly a small fish flies out of the water and into a bird's nest in a tree; then it jumps back into the water. Write more about what your experience might be like with this mysterious flying fish.

 Have you ever gone without TV for more than a few days? What kinds of things might you do if you were not allowed to watch your favorite television programs for an entire week?

AUGUST

August 17

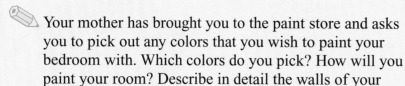

The carnival is in town and there is a new ride called the Death Valley Sidewinder. Write what you'd say to your parents to persuade them to let you go on this ride.

Your mother has brought you to the paint store and asks you to pick out any colors that you wish to paint your bedroom with. Which colors do you pick? How will you paint your room? Describe in detail the walls of your newly painted bedroom.

August 18

The town council is about to adopt a new ordinance to ban skateboarding along the town's streets. Write a letter to the editor protesting the proposed ordinance.

The school board is planning to install metal detectors at all entrances to your school. Write what you'd say to the school board if you were asked to give your opinion about the installation of the detectors.

August 19

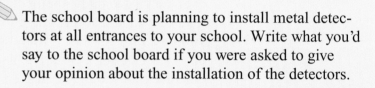

Today is National Aviation Day and the birthday of Orville Wright. Pretend you are watching the Wright brothers complete the first successful flight of an airplane and describe what you see.

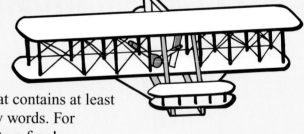

Today is the birthday of poet Ogden Nash. In remembrance of this writer, compose a poem that contains at least one witty comparison and a few invented or silly words. For example, you might compare your little brother to a frog!

August 20

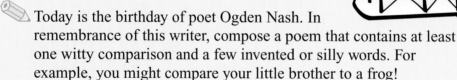
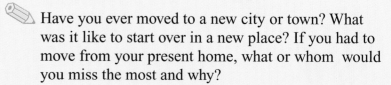

Have you ever been asked to keep a secret? Did you keep it? Describe what it felt like to know a secret but not be able to tell anyone about it.

Have you ever moved to a new city or town? What was it like to start over in a new place? If you had to move from your present home, what or whom would you miss the most and why?

August 21

On this day in 1959, Hawaii became the 50th state of the United States. If there could be a 51st state, what would you like it to be? Write a letter to your congressman stating your choice and the reasons why you think it should be named the 51st state.

If you had to choose, would you rather be rich or famous? If you'd rather be rich, how would you spend your money? If you'd rather be famous, what would you like to be famous for?

August 22

Pretend you're a contestant on a kid's game show. As the loser of the first round of questions, you have a choice of being dropped into a giant bowl of chocolate pudding or having a dozen eggs dropped on your head. Which would you choose and why? Describe what happens and what it feels like for the option you choose.

If you could create your own summer resort, what would you call it, where would it be located, and what type of resort would it be?

August 23

Have you ever listened to the birds chirping outside? What words do their noises resemble? Write down a pretend conversation that two or more birds might be having outside your window.

While scuba diving off the coast of Brazil, you find a rare Spanish coin and bring it to the surface. Your friends dive in after you and find several more. Briefly explain where you think these unusual coins came from and how they ended up at the bottom of the ocean.

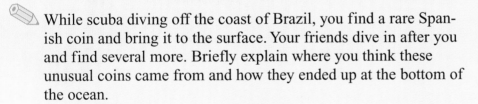

August 24

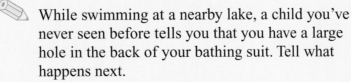

If there could only be one law in the United States, what should it be? Why?

While swimming at a nearby lake, a child you've never seen before tells you that you have a large hole in the back of your bathing suit. Tell what happens next.

August 25

A plant in your backyard is growing black boots instead of leaves. Explain what you plan to do with this unusual plant.

If you had a videotape of every funny thing that's happened to you or someone you know, which clip or scene would you send to a funny home-video television program? Why?

August 26

Imagine that you wake up one day and find that you can no longer speak English! You are now speaking some unknown language that no one understands. Describe what happens next and how you plan on getting your old language back.

For many families, it is now back-to-school shopping time. What kinds of clothes are popular among your friends? What styles are not popular?

August 27

A spaceship is hovering above your house and beams you up inside the craft! The aliens inside the ship tell you that you have been chosen as the leader of their planet, Zok. You are crowned King Dribblebib and fly away into space. Describe how you react and what happens next.

Tell the story of a new baseball legend named Crush Baynes who practices his home run swing by swatting hailstones during thunderstorms! Include as many details as possible about this tall tale of a baseball player.

August 28

Pretend that for ten seconds a tornado takes you for a ride before dropping you safely into a large pile of hay. Describe your ten-second adventure inside the tornado.

Pretend that you have an identical twin and you switch places for the day. Describe what it's like to be your sibling for a day.

August 29

✎ Your Uncle Jeb has invited you to spend a few days working with him on his farm. Tell what happens from the moment you get there until you say good-bye.

✎ Your mother has just been elected president of the United States! Describe what you are thinking as you pack your things for the White House.

August 30

✎ Imagine that all the animals in a local zoo have escaped and are stampeding through your town! Describe how you plan on saving the town without hurting the animals.

✎ You've been asked to baby-sit for a neighbor's pesky three-year-old for two hours. Describe how you win over the child and become buddies in only two hours.

August 31

✎ Complete the following story: On our bus ride to school, we noticed the driver looking pale and drowsy. Before we knew it, he was fast asleep!

✎ You have just returned home from school and find a kid named Jack sitting in your room and holding a goose. The only other strange thing you find in your room is an opened book of fairy tales. Explain where the boy came from and how you plan to get him back there.

September 1

 The wreckage of the "unsinkable" Titanic was found on this day in 1985. Write about a time when you were just sure a plan would work out, but it didn't.

 Your best friend moved away over the summer. Write your friend a letter describing the first day of school without her. How is this year different than last?

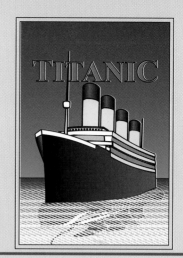

September 2

 Thomas Farrinor, the baker for England's King Charles II, is remembered for starting the Great Fire of London in 1666 when he forgot to turn off his oven. Is it better to be famous for something bad or to not be famous at all? Explain your answer.

 Introduce yourself to your classmates by writing a paragraph about the three things you would like them to know about you.

September 3

 September is National Self-Improvement Month. If you could change just one thing about yourself, what would it be? How would the change be an improvement?

 If "dog days" are the hot days of summer, what would "rabbit days" be? And what about "snake days"? Choose an animal and describe the kind of weather that should bear that animal's name.

so I said...

September 4

 Ten-year-old Barney Flaherty became the first newsboy on this day in 1833. If you could have an after-school job, what would you do with your earnings?

 Eavesdrop on an imaginary conversation that's going on between items in your bookbag or desk. What are your belongings saying to each other?

September 5

Tick Tock Tick Tock

Today is Be Late for Something Day. Which saying describes you better: "A Stitch in Time Saves Nine," or "Better Late Than Never"? Explain why.

A pencil is having a conversation with a piece of paper at the end of the first week of school. What are these two school supplies saying to each other?

September 6

Celebrate National Do It Day by writing a plan to accomplish something you've been putting off. Be sure to include a deadline for completing your plan. Good luck!

Pretend you are a passenger on the first westbound train to arrive in San Francisco on this date in 1869. What is your opinion of this new "modern" mode of transportation?

September 7

The first Miss America Pageant began today in 1921. How do you define beauty?

September is National School Success Month. What "ingredients" do you think go into success? Use the ingredients to write a recipe for the most successful school year ever.

September 8

The first Sunday after Labor Day is National Grandparents Day. Write a letter to a grandparent or an older person who means a lot to you. Tell this person what makes him or her so special.

The first days of school can cause a young student anxiety. Write a letter to a new kindergarten student which puts him at ease and gives him a few pointers on how to succeed in school.

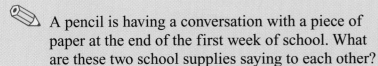

SEPTEMBER

September 9

 September 9 is Teddy Bear Day. Write a letter to your childhood teddy bear or other cuddly friend telling it why it was so special to you.

 Write a story that begins with "It all started when I poured orange juice on my cornflakes."

September 10

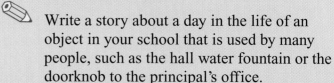 Today is Hot Dog Day. Write a story about a time when you were a real hot dog in a game or with your friends. What did you learn from the experience?

 Write a story about a day in the life of an object in your school that is used by many people, such as the hall water fountain or the doorknob to the principal's office.

September 11

 September is National Chicken Month. Write a story that explains how a coward came to be called "chicken."

 Your teacher could not come to school today. Instead, she sent a note to you asking *you* to be the substitute. What will you do with the class today?

September 12

 The third week in September is National Courtesy Week. To celebrate, write a story in which every time the main character is courteous to someone, something good happens to her.

 World Gratitude Day is observed in September. For whom or what are you most grateful? Explain.

Thank You!

September 13

 New York City became the first capital of the United States on this date in 1788, years before Washington, DC, became home to the nation's federal government. Write a letter to the president telling him why your hometown should be the nation's next capital.

 Describe writer's block as if it were a monster. Then share a trick or two for taming this creativity-crunching creature.

September 14

 September is Read-a-New-Book Month. Write about a book that you would like to read that hasn't been written yet.

Complete the following sentence: "In the first few weeks of school, I have learned..."

September 15

 An unofficial American flag, flown on this day in 1775, had the word *Liberty* spelled on a dark blue background. Describe a new flag for today's America and tell what each color and symbol represents.

Pretend that your community is considering extending the school week to include a half day on Saturday! Is this a good idea? Write a letter to the school board expressing your opinion and explaining your reasons.

September 16

 Today is magician David Copperfield's birthday. While you are attending a party in his honor, you find a magic mirror that shows you what you will be in the future. What do you see?

Substitute Teacher Appreciation Week is in September. Pretend you are a substitute teacher and write a story about how the other kids would treat you if you were their teacher.

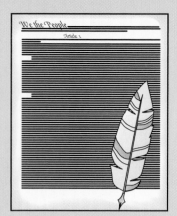

September 17

 Only 38 of the 41 delegates attending the Constitutional Convention in 1787 actually signed the Constitution. Pretend you are a signing delegate. Write a letter to one of the three non-signing delegates. What can you say to convince them to sign?

 Your teacher sends you to the supply closet for staples. Just as you reach for a box, you discover that the closet is really a time-travel machine! Where and when does it take you? What do you see while you're there?

September 18

 Today is the birthday of Samuel Johnson, creator of the first true dictionary of the English language. Choose a word you think should be used more often; then write a commercial to convince your classmates to use the word more.

 Are you an early bird or a night owl? What changes need to be made in the school schedule so that it fits your style?

September 19

 National Student Day, a day to encourage students to do well in school and go on to college, is celebrated in September. What would you like to be when you grow up? What will you do to prepare for your chosen career?

 Your school is planning a parade for American Heritage Month and each class is to have its own float. Describe the float you would design for your class.

September 20

 The Equal Rights Party nominated Belva Ann Lockwood as their candidate for the U.S. presidency on this date in 1884. She was not elected. Do you think the qualifications for a woman to be a leader should be different from those for a man? Explain your answer.

 You have just been told that a substitute will teach your class tomorrow. Help the substitute out by writing directions on how to find her way around your classroom.

September 21

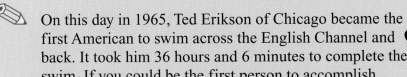

September is All-American Breakfast Month. Write a how-to paragraph that gives step-by-step instructions of how to prepare your favorite breakfast food.

On this day in 1965, Ted Erikson of Chicago became the first American to swim across the English Channel and back. It took him 36 hours and 6 minutes to complete the swim. If you could be the first person to accomplish something great, what would it be? Explain your answer.

September 22

Today is Dear Diary Day. Beginning with the words "Dear Diary," write about a day so wacky that it could never happen in real life! Or...could it?

It is very late at night and the phone rings unexpectedly. Who is it? Why are they calling? What happens next?

September 23

Today is the first full day of autumn. How will you "turn over a new leaf" this school year?

Chocolate-covered green beans? Oatmeal with chocolate sauce? What food tastes so bad to you that it could only be saved by the addition of chocolate? Create a menu full of chocolate-covered taste creations in honor of National Chocolate Day.

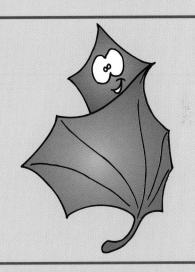

September 24

Time for my flea bath!

The last full week in September is National Dog Week. If dogs could talk, what do you think they would say about this honor? Write an imaginary conversation between two dogs discussing how they plan to celebrate National Dog Week.

If you changed colors as your moods change, the way leaves change colors in the fall, how often would you change? What colors would you be?

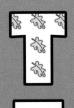

September 25

 Today is the anniversary of the first baseball doubleheader, which was played in 1882. Pretend you are a baseball and describe what it's like to be in a game.

 Make up a story about what's really on the other side of the faculty lounge door! Where do your teachers *really* go on break and what do they do when they get there?

September 26

 Celebrate Good Neighbor Day by nominating someone who lives or sits near you as "Neighbor of the Year." Write a paragraph explaining your choice.

 If everything you owned had to be the same color, what color would you choose? Why?

September 27

 The fourth Friday in September is Native American Day. Pretend you are a Native American child who has never seen the white sails of a European ship. What do you think about as the first ship glides into view?

 Pretend that the lines on your paper are really the closed slats of a window blind! What wonderful (or terrible) surprise is on the other side?

September 28

 Today is Ask a Stupid Question Day. If you could ask any question without anyone thinking it was stupid, what would your question be? Who would you ask?

 Today is the birthday of Chinese philosopher Confucius. *Philosophy* comes from two Greek words meaning "love" and "wisdom." Using this definition of the word, are you a *philosopher*? Why or why not?

September 29

Lunch

✎ September is Youth Month. Describe what it is like being a kid in your family. Are you the youngest? Oldest? What are the advantages and disadvantages of your age?

✎ Everyone overslept this morning and you had to pack your own school lunch! Your mom told you to pack anything you wanted. Describe what you packed.

September 30

✎ The first book was printed on this date in 1452. How would your education be different if there were no books?

✎ Fall is a time for animals to prepare for the winter. Some store extra food. Some grow warm fur coats. How do you get ready for winter?

October 1

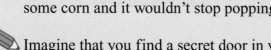 October is National Popcorn Poppin' Month. Write a story about what would happen if you were popping some corn and it wouldn't stop popping!

Imagine that you find a secret door in your classroom. Explain what happens once you open it.

October 2

 Charlie Brown®, Snoopy®, and the rest of the PEANUTS® comic strip gang celebrate their anniversary today. Create a new character for this comic strip, or create your own new comic strip.

If a desk could talk, what would it say about its previous students and classes? Write a dialogue between you and your desk.

October 3

 The first week of October is No Salt Week. Describe what eating food would be like if there were no seasonings.

Pretend that your home has suddenly turned into a giant pumpkin. Describe how your life would be different inside your new home.

October 4

 Fire Prevention Week occurs during the month of October. Many families use this time to plan a fire escape route in their homes. Choose the most difficult room in your house to escape from and describe your route to safety.

Your school has girls who want to play on the boys' football team. Write arguments for or against this issue, making sure to defend your reasons with concrete support.

October 5

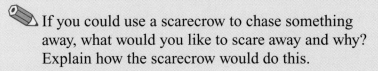 The first Monday of October is known as Children's Day. Your principal has asked you to organize this year's celebration. What kinds of things will you do to celebrate Children's Day?

If you could use a scarecrow to chase something away, what would you like to scare away and why? Explain how the scarecrow would do this.

October 6

The first week in October is Universal Children's Week. In honor of this occasion, write an essay about how important children are to the future of our planet.

Pretend that you could be the teacher for a day. Describe what the day would be like.

October 7

October is National Pizza Month. Celebrate by writing a "pizza poem" describing your favorite flavor of this special Italian pie.

If you could plan a class field trip to anywhere, where would you go and what would happen there?

Next stop – Mars!

October 8

October is National Stamp Collecting Month. If you could choose any person to be on the next postage stamp, who would it be and why?

You have learned many things since you began school. Write about one thing you learned in kindergarten that you have used this year.

33¢

October 9

 National Newspaper Week is celebrated during the second week of October. Write a headline and newspaper story about the worst grade you ever received on a test. Be sure to include *who, what, when, where,* and *why.*

Describe the perfect camping trip. Include details about where you are, who is with you, and what you have on hand for supplies.

October 10

 National Pet Peeve Week is celebrated annually during the second full week of October. Think about the one thing that really drives you crazy. Then write a persuasive letter to your pet peeve asking it to change and become less annoying.

Think of a person who has a very positive attitude toward school, sports, home, or any other aspect of life. What could you do to be more like this person and have a more positive attitude about any or all of the things listed above?

October 11

 Eleanor Roosevelt, our country's first lady from 1933–1945, was born on October 11, 1884. First ladies become almost as famous as their presidential husbands. How do you think it would feel to be as famous as the president or the first lady?

Pretend you are in a hot-air balloon hovering above your school or neighborhood. Describe what you see.

October 12

 October is National Youth Against Tobacco Month. Write a persuasive letter to someone who is thinking about smoking for the first time. In your letter, tell this person why you think smoking is such a bad idea.

 What if our government started using candy instead of money? What candy do you think should be used as the $100 bill? Explain why.

October 13

✏️ Some people have a fear of the number 13, which is called *triskaidekaphobia.* Name something you're afraid of and explain why. How do you deal with this fear?

✏️ Imagine that you are a ball on the playground. Naturally, you are very popular at recess! Describe who plays with you and how you are treated.

October 14

✏️ John F. Kennedy, who was about to become president, first spoke about the Peace Corps on this day in 1960. What does *peace* mean to you? How do you think our country should go about obtaining it?

✏️ Imagine that you have been hired by Milton Bradley to create a new game. Describe your new creation and explain why you think it would be a best-seller.

October 15

✏️ October 15 is National Grouch Day. List ten things that make you grouchy.

✏️ Your best friend takes you to a secret cave. After you explore for a while, your flashlights go out. Explain what happens next.

October 16

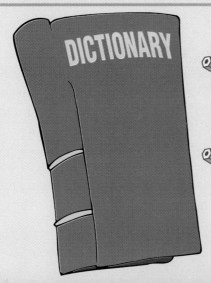

✏️ Dictionary Day honors the birthday of Noah Webster. If you could create a brand-new word, what would it be and what would it mean?

✏️ Imagine that you tune into the evening news just in time to hear your name mentioned! Write about the news event you were involved in.

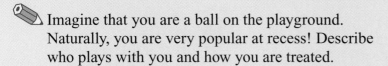

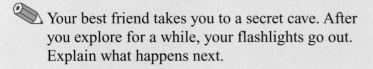
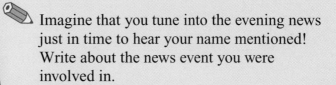

October 17

 National School Bus Safety Week is the third full week in October. Describe a school bus of the future that comes complete with several new safety features of your own invention.

 You have just raked all the fall leaves in your yard into one big pile. Suddenly something starts to crawl out from inside the pile. Describe what happens next.

October 18

 October 18 is Alaska Day. Write a poem in this state's honor. For a chilly challenge, make all the lines rhyme with *ice*.

 Pretend that an ordinary object—such as a bed, a desk, or a bike—is suddenly made out of marshmallows. Write a story explaining what happens next.

October 19

 October 19 is Evaluate Your Life Day. Write about something you've always wanted to do with your life but haven't gotten around to yet. Then list some ways in which you might realistically reach your goal.

 Imagine that you won first prize in a contest you entered. Write about your winning entry and describe your fabulous prize.

FIRST PRIZE

Hasn't she ever heard of tuna fish?

October 20

 National Business Women's Week begins on the third Monday in October. Write a letter to your favorite woman describing a new business venture that would be perfect for her.

 Write about a day in the life of your pet from his point of view. Include information on his feelings about various aspects of his day.

October 21

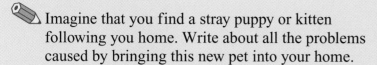

🖊️ October is National Roller Skating Month. Write a poem or story that takes place in a roller-skating rink.

🖊️ Imagine that you find a stray puppy or kitten following you home. Write about all the problems caused by bringing this new pet into your home.

October 22

🖊️ Family History Month is observed in October. What are some of the crazy things your family has done to go down in history?

🖊️ You decide that there should be two of you, so you have yourself cloned. Explain what a few typical days would be like in your lives.

October 23

🖊️ Michael Crichton celebrates his birthday on this day. Crichton wrote the book *Jurassic Park,* on which the popular movie and its sequel were based. Why do you think people are still so fascinated with dinosaurs?

🖊️ Write about an embarrassing moment in your life. Tell about who else was involved and how you recovered from your embarrassment.

October 24

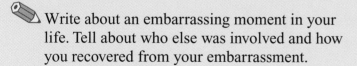

🖊️ Write a story that ends with the following sentence: "From now on, I'll keep that door locked!"

🖊️ Imagine that you are a squirrel gathering nuts for the winter. Describe your best hiding places. Explain what happened last year when you forgot where you buried the seeds and nuts!

OCTOBER

October 25

Look around you to see how many signs of autumn you can see. Choose one or two of the signs and describe them completely. Include as many of the senses as you can in your description.

Grandparents can teach us a lot. Write about what you might eventually be able to teach *your* grandchildren.

October 26

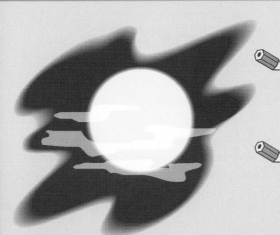

The last week in October is known as Peace, Friendship and Good Will Week. Choose a friend and write him a letter telling him how much he means to you.

People often talk about how a full moon affects people's behavior. Write a story about how the full moon once affected you or someone you know.

October 27

National Pork Month is celebrated in October. Pretend you are a pig and write a letter to the president persuading him to change October to National Poultry Month instead!

If you won a contest that allowed you to appear on any TV show, which show would it be? Describe what would happen on the show during your appearance.

October 28

October is International Fired Up Month. Write about some of the things you do to get fired up before sporting events or extracurricular activities.

Imagine that a thunderstorm starts just as you are walking home from a friend's house. There is lightning and thunder, and suddenly all the lights in the nearby houses go out. Explain what happens next.

October 29

The early bird gets the best costume! Only two days left until Halloween, and you have just discovered that all the stores are sold out of costumes. Design a costume you make from scratch using only items you can find around your house.

If you could put on a magic hat and become anyone in the world, who would you become and why?

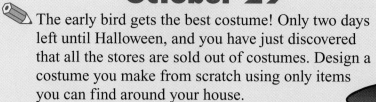

October 30

Think of something that makes you feel scared. Make up a story to explain why this brings you so much fear.

Pretend you are given the power to change places with a fairy tale character. Tell which character you would trade places with and how you might change your part in the story.

October 31

Imagine that after trick-or-treating on Halloween you can't take your costume off! Write about what happens at school the next day.

Houdini, the great magician and escape artist, died on this day. If you could escape from any container, what container would you choose, and how would you complete the escape?

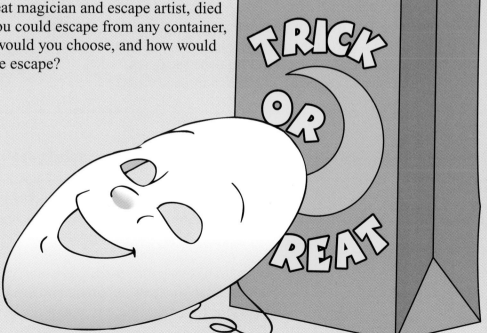

NOVEMBER

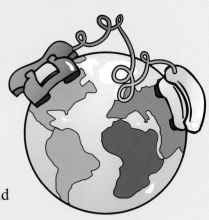

November 1

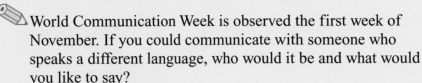

Today is National Author's Day. To celebrate, write a letter to the author of your favorite book. Include a description of a story you'd like to see made into a book.

World Communication Week is observed the first week of November. If you could communicate with someone who speaks a different language, who would it be and what would you like to say?

November 2

The Mrs. America beauty pageant began on this date in 1988. Write a letter to the sponsors of the pageant nominating a mother you know as the next Mrs. America. Why is she the perfect choice?

Do you like where you live? Voice your opinion by writing a letter to a local official in which you describe what would make your neighborhood or community a better place to live.

November 3

On this day in 1957, a female dog named Laika became the first living creature to orbit the earth! Write a story about an exceptional pet you have known or one that you would like to know.

Sandwich Day is celebrated on this day in November. List all the different ingredients you think would be needed to make "A Successful Student Sandwich," such as "one slice of courage" and "a dab of dedication."

November 4

Thank You!

National Card and Letter Writing Week is held each year in November. Write a letter to your teacher telling him how you have benefited from being in his class so far this year.

Take me to your leader! Write a list of all the things you think it takes to make a good leader. Now rank the items from the most important to the least important and discuss why you put them in that order.

November 5

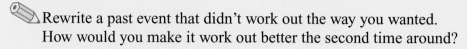

✏️ Guy Fawkes Day celebrates Britain's most notorious traitor. Describe how you might feel if your best friend betrayed you.

✏️ Rewrite a past event that didn't work out the way you wanted. How would you make it work out better the second time around?

November 6

✏️ Today marks the birth anniversary of Adolphe Sax, a Belgian musician who invented the saxophone. If you could choose any musical instrument to play, which one would it be and why?

✏️ Observe Cat Week, the first full week in November, by making a list of idioms and proverbs that include the word *cat,* such as "He let the cat out of the bag." Then explain what each phrase means.

November 7

✏️ The first international soccer match was played during this month in 1872. Today, soccer is the world's most popular sport. Describe a game that might have the honor of being the most popular sport 100 years from today.

✏️ Today marks the halfway point of autumn. If you could choose one of the four seasons to last all year long, which would you choose? Why?

November 8

✏️ November is Good Nutrition Month. Write a persuasive paragraph explaining the importance of healthful eating.

✏️ Write a letter to put in your school's cafeteria suggestion box. What suggestions can you make to improve both the nutrition and the taste of your school's meals?

November 9

 Today marks the anniversary of the East Coast Blackout which occurred in 1965. More than 30 million people over an area of 80,000 square miles were without power. How would you survive if you were caught in a power outage?

Write an original story that ends with the line, "Now you know why there are so many stars in the sky."

November 10

 Forget-Me-Not Day is celebrated in November. Write about someone who you hope will never forget you.

The windshield wiper was patented on this day in 1903. What problem in today's world would you like to "wipe out" forever? Why does this problem bother you?

November 11

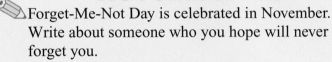 Veterans Day, observed annually on November 11, is a day to honor all the veterans of the U.S. armed forces. What do you think is the best way to honor our veterans?

Pretend you are a tree. Write a story about what changes you must go through from autumn to winter.

November 12

 Write a story about what might have happened if Cinderella hadn't lost her shoe in the famous fairy tale.

Pretend you have found a postage stamp that will carry a letter back in time. Whom will you write? What will you say?

November 13

Robert Louis Stevenson, author of *Treasure Island,* was born on this day in 1850. As a young boy, Stevenson was often too sickly to attend school, so he would write stories to entertain himself. What do you do to amuse yourself when you are too sick to go to school?

Look around the room and choose an item. Then write a paragraph that describes the item so well that a classmate can identify the item without actually seeing it.

November 14

In 1862, Lewis Carroll kept his promise to a little girl named Alice and began writing the story that later became known as *Alice in Wonderland.* Write about a time when someone made you feel special by keeping a promise.

Imagine you are the very last leaf on a tree. Write a story describing how you feel.

November 15

"Eat Pat!"

Today is *Shichi-Go-San* in Japan, a festival during which children who are three, five, and seven years old are honored as lucky. The children dress in their finest clothes and receive gifts of candy and toys. Create a holiday honoring children of your age. What might happen on this special day?

Pretend you are Tom the Turkey. Write a paragraph persuading people to eat Pat the Pig for Thanksgiving dinner instead!

November 16

Today marks the birth anniversary of children's author Jean Fritz. Her books include fictional stories based on real historical events. If you could be a fly on the wall at any historical event, which event would you choose and why?

Today is National Fast Food Day. To celebrate, create a menu for a new fast-food restaurant. Be sure to include items from each of the four food groups.

N O V E M B E R

November 17

✎ Mark Twain once said, "Never let school get in the way of your education." Describe a lesson you've learned outside school either alone or with someone's help.

✎ Poof! While eating a piece of leftover Halloween candy, you are magically turned into a turkey just in time for Thanksgiving! How will you convince your family not to have you for Thanksgiving dinner?

November 18

✎ Mickey® Mouse's birthday is on November 18. Make a list of the benefits of watching cartoons. Now make a list of the disadvantages. Decide which list is longer and then explain why you think that is.

✎ Today is the birthday of Louis Daguerre, the inventor of the daguerreotype photographic process. Write about an event in your life that was "picture-perfect."

November 19

✎ Today is the birthday of James Garfield, the first left-handed U.S. president. In honor of the occasion, write a note to your best friend using your left hand. (If you are left-handed, write a note using your right hand.) Then give yourself a left-handed pat on the back if he can actually read it!

✎ While playing on the playground, you notice a small book in the snow. Upon opening it, you find it's a Passport to the Impossible, allowing you to travel to a place that you could have never visited before. Describe your destination and what you learn while you are there.

November 20

✎ Celebrate Absurdity Day by writing a story that begins at the end and moves backward to "Once upon a time…"

✎ Rights of the Child Day is observed on November 20. What rights do you think all children should have?

November 21

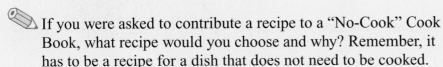

World Hello Day is held in November. Celebrate by writing a friendly letter introducing yourself to someone from another country.

If you were asked to contribute a recipe to a "No-Cook" Cook Book, what recipe would you choose and why? Remember, it has to be a recipe for a dish that does not need to be cooked.

November 22

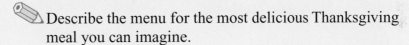

Today is Start Your Own Country Day. Imagine a country inhabited by people who are happiest when they are *un*happy. Describe what a "good" day would be like in this country.

Describe the menu for the most delicious Thanksgiving meal you can imagine.

November 23

Commemorate National Cashew Day by writing a story which begins with the line, "Sometimes I feel like a nut…."

Create a new mascot for your favorite sports team. What does it look like? What does it eat, wear, and do?

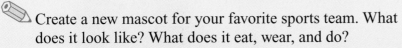

November 24

If you could set an extra plate for dinner and invite anyone you wanted, whom would you invite and why? Write an invitation to this person telling him all the important information about the meal.

Design a parade float which accurately represents your school. Describe the float, how it's decorated, and what symbols are used to represent your school.

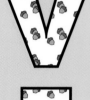

November 25

Many retail stores run large sales the day after Thanksgiving. Instead of hitting the sales this year, celebrate Buy Nothing Day by not spending any money. How many ways can you think of to spend time at the mall without buying anything at all?

Describe a gift you could make with materials found lying around your house.

November 26

Peanut butter on spaghetti? Peanut butter–flavored soft drinks? Celebrate Peanut Butter Lovers' Month by creating a wacky new recipe for a food made using peanut butter!

Most schools close for a few days around special holidays. Does yours? Describe a typical vacation day spent away from school.

November 27

On this day in 1779, America's first university was formally established in Pennsylvania. Do you think a college degree is necessary to succeed in today's world? Explain your answer.

Close your eyes and travel back in time to the most rotten day you've ever experienced. Looking back on the day now, what are some ways you could have changed it to make it turn out better?

November 28

Write a story titled "That Was Then, This Is Now" in which you compare yourself today to yourself at this time last year.

What kind of sense of humor do you have? Describe an incident that illustrates your sense of humor.

November 29

 Today is the birthday of Louisa May Alcott, author of *Little Men* and *Little Women*. She wrote these books based on her own family experiences. Write a story about your family.

A new student has just joined your class. Help this student adjust to a new school by writing a detailed list of the events that occur during a typical day in your classroom.

Class Schedule

7:55 Bell Rings
8:00 Teacher takes
      up lunch money
8:15 Pledge of
      Allegiance
8:20 Show and Tell

November 30

Samuel Clemens was born on this day in 1835. Clemens, the author known as Mark Twain, chose his pen name based on a riverboat term meaning *two fathoms*. Choose a pen name for yourself and explain why you chose it.

Pretend you are a snowflake falling to the ground. Describe your airborne adventure.

NOVEMBER

December 1

 Choose your favorite children's book. Now write a different ending to it.

 December 1 is World AIDS Day. What would you say to a loved one who has developed AIDS?

December 2

Imagine that you are the star player on your favorite sports team. Describe the most exciting part of a recent game.

Every sports team needs enthusiastic fans and cheer-leaders. Write a cheer to inspire your favorite sports team to victory.

December 3

Although December is the 12th month on our calendar, it was the 10th month on the early Roman calendar. Imagine that you could schedule the months in any order. What order would you choose? Why?

 During the first week of each December, New York City begins the holiday season by lighting the giant Christmas tree at Rockefeller Center. What event marks the beginning of the holiday season for you?

December 4

 December is Universal Human Rights Month. What three rights do you think all people should have?

 While no two snowflakes are alike, all snowflakes share certain characteristics. For example, all snow-flakes have six sides. In what ways are snowflakes like people?

December 5

Animator and filmmaker Walt Disney was born on this day in 1901. Which Disney movie or character is your favorite? Why?

Big news—one of Santa's reindeer has decided to retire! To help Santa choose a replacement, describe the qualities that make a good reindeer for Santa's sleigh.

December 6

Bears hibernate during the winter. This means that the bears are in an inactive, sleeplike state. If humans hibernated during the winter, how would your neighborhood, town, or city be different?

Pretend that you are in charge of planning a special dinner for your family tonight. What would be on the menu? How would you prepare for the meal?

December 7

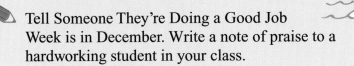

Have you ever heard of the Polar Bear Club? This club is for people who like to swim in icy waters during cold winter months. Many people who share interests or hobbies form clubs. If you were to form a club, what would it be?

Tell Someone They're Doing a Good Job Week is in December. Write a note of praise to a hardworking student in your class.

December 8

John Lennon, a member of the rock group The Beatles, died on this day in 1980. Many of The Beatles' songs are still popular today. Do you think any of your favorite songs will still be popular in 30 years? Tell which ones and why.

Pretend that your bed can fly. Where would it take you? Describe what you would see.

December 9

 Wow! Two feet of snow fell last night, and now school has been canceled. As you look out your bedroom window, you see a lost polar bear trudging through the snow. Write about what happens next.

 In Sweden, there's a hotel that's made out of some very unusual materials—snow and ice! Describe what it would be like to visit a hotel like this.

December 10

Christmas
Kwanzaa
Hanukkah

 List as many holidays as you can that take place in December.

 Each December, Nobel Prizes are awarded on this day. Each winner will receive a large cash prize. What global problem would you spend your prize money to solve? Explain.

December 11

 Have you surfed the Internet? Think of a Web site that you like. If you created your own Web site, what would you include?

 December is Safe Toys and Gifts Month. What toys on the market do you think are unsafe? What would you do to improve the safety level of one of these toys?

December 12

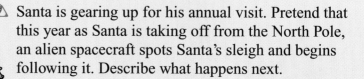

During this time of year many people bake cookies and make candy to share with family and friends. Make a list of your favorite holiday foods.

Santa is gearing up for his annual visit. Pretend that this year as Santa is taking off from the North Pole, an alien spacecraft spots Santa's sleigh and begins following it. Describe what happens next.

December 13

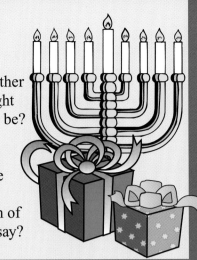

✎ During Hanukkah, Jewish families light a candle and give each other a gift each night for eight nights. If you were to give someone eight special gifts, to whom would you give them and what would they be?

✎ As you are looking at an old scrapbook, you discover a letter written to your great-great-grandmother from President Theodore Roosevelt. The letter is dated December 13, 1901. Roosevelt had been president for about three months following the assassination of President William McKinley in September. What does the letter say?

December 14

✎ On December 14, 1798, David Wilkinson of Rhode Island received a patent for the first nut-and-bolt machine. What's one thing that really drives you nuts? Explain.

✎ Nostradamus, a French doctor, was born on this day in 1503. He is famous for his astrological predictions. Many people believe his predictions foretold the future. Write your predictions for the coming year.

December 15

...in-line skates, a video game, some CDs...

✎ Make a list of gifts that you would like to receive. Which is your favorite? Explain at least one way that you could share this gift with someone else.

✎ Many people visit their relatives during the holidays. Pretend that your uncle has just stopped by to visit, and he has brought a famous person as a surprise. Who is it? How does your family react?

December 16

✎ Eat What You Want Day is observed on this date each year. To celebrate, create a mouthwatering menu for breakfast, lunch, and dinner.

✎ The Safe Drinking Water Act became law on this day in 1974. Why is it important to have a law protecting our water supply?

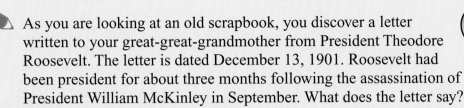

December 17

 In December 1929, Edwin S. Lowe manufactured the first bingo game. What is your favorite game? What changes would you make to improve the rules of this game?

 List the letters in *December* in a column. Write a word that describes December for each letter.

B	I	N	G	O
29	60	8	43	12
13	32	27	55	34
48	11	Free Space	21	36
5	17	29	78	89
94	62	73	18	40

December 18

 You've just put the finishing touches on the best snowman that you've ever built. Suddenly your snowman comes alive! Describe what happens next.

 Many birds fly south during the winter. Pretend you are a bird flying south. Write your own bird's-eye view of the trip.

December 19

 Sometimes a heavy snowfall causes an *avalanche:* a mass of snow that slides down a mountain slope. Pretend you are a snowflake caught in an avalanche. Describe the experience.

Many families have holiday traditions. Write about one of your family traditions that is special to you.

December 20

 When the temperature falls below 32° F, water freezes. Describe what it would be like if the streets and sidewalks in your neighborhood were covered with ice all year long.

Get ready early and make a New Year's resolution. Write down something you want to change or improve about yourself.

December 21

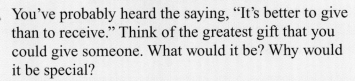

You've probably heard the saying, "It's better to give than to receive." Think of the greatest gift that you could give someone. What would it be? Why would it be special?

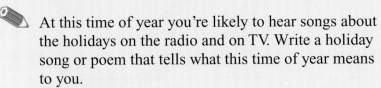

At this time of year you're likely to hear songs about the holidays on the radio and on TV. Write a holiday song or poem that tells what this time of year means to you.

December 22

Winter has begun! Depending on where you live, you may be wearing sweaters, heavy jackets, scarves, and gloves to keep warm. Describe your favorite winter outfit.

In the wintertime many people enjoy skiing, ice skating, and sledding. What winter sports are popular in your area? Write about a time when you participated in one of these sports.

December 23

At this time of year many students enjoy a winter vacation that lasts about two weeks. What will you do during that time? Write about your plans.

In some places ice fishing is a popular winter sport. Pretend that you and a friend are at a frozen lake. You have cut a small hole in the ice and lowered your fishing line into the water below. Describe what happens next.

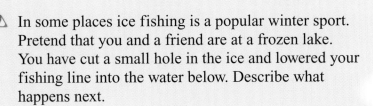

December 24

In December 1913, the first crossword puzzle was published in the *New York World* newspaper. If you could write a weekly newspaper column titled "Just For Kids," what topics would you include and why?

Mistletoe is an evergreen plant with tiny yellow flowers. One holiday tradition is that if you get caught standing under mistletoe you will get a kiss from someone. If you could start a new holiday tradition, what would it be?

December 25

Today is Christmas, a day when Christians celebrate the birth of Christ, give gifts, and visit family and friends. Describe what it would be like if every day were Christmas.

Clara Barton, the founder of the American Red Cross, was born on this day in 1821. What qualities do you think a person should have in order to serve as a disaster relief volunteer?

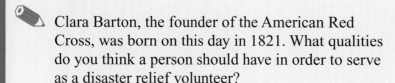

December 26

Today is Boxing Day in Britain, Australia, Canada, and New Zealand. On this day people traditionally give gifts to charities and to those in need. Describe a time when you gave a gift or did a good deed for someone in need.

On the day after Christmas, many people go shopping to return gifts that are too big, too small, the wrong color, or just not quite right. Have you ever returned a gift? Explain why. If not, describe a gift that you wish you could have returned.

December 27

What is your favorite holiday movie, TV show, or book? Why? Describe the story.

Kwanzaa began yesterday and ends on January 1. This holiday celebrates African-American culture and focuses on seven traditional African principles. The first principle that's emphasized is unity. What is unity? Why is it important for a family or community?

December 28

Today is the birthday of Woodrow Wilson—well, maybe. Historians aren't sure whether Wilson was born on December 28 or December 29. If you could pick any day to be your birthday, what day would you choose? Why?

Imagine that you are a snowman in your front yard. Describe what you see happening around you.

December 29

You are standing in line at the supermarket when a reindeer walks into the store! Describe what happens next.

Cellist Pablo Casals was born on this day in 1876. He became an accomplished musician at an early age. What two things would you like to accomplish before you are 16?

December 30

Some writers become famous for writing about unusual places or places that they know well. Choose a place that you know well and that you think others would like to read about. Describe it.

Write a description of a family member or friend. Include not only what that person looks like, but also what kind of person he or she is.

December 31

In 1999 many people worried that the Y2K computer problem would cause the world's computers to stop working on January 1. Imagine that all computers stopped working tomorrow. Write about what you think would happen.

You're All Done Day is observed on this date each year. It is a day to celebrate the past year's accomplishments and the satisfaction of a job well done. What personal accomplishment of this year are you most proud of? Why?

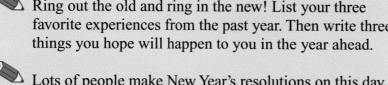

January 1

Ring out the old and ring in the new! List your three favorite experiences from the past year. Then write three things you hope will happen to you in the year ahead.

Lots of people make New Year's resolutions on this day. Many times people's New Year's resolutions deal with improving themselves in some way. Write a paragraph describing one thing you would like to improve about yourself.

January 2

Dinosaur Days

33¢

On this date in 1893, the U.S. Post Office issued the first commemorative postage stamp. It honored the 400th anniversary of the discovery of America. Imagine you've designed a special stamp. Describe it.

In many places January is one of the coldest months of the year. Imagine that it started snowing in your town on January 2 and didn't stop until January 31! Describe what life would be like in your town with this much snow.

January 3

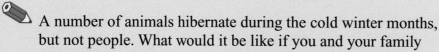

Alaska became the 49th state on this date in 1959. Alaska is also home to some very unusual animals. Imagine, on a trip to Alaska, you encounter a polar bear! What will you do? How will you get away or make the polar bear go away?

A number of animals hibernate during the cold winter months, but not people. What would it be like if you and your family had to hibernate during the winter? Write about what you and your family would need to do to prepare for such a long sleep.

January 4

Jakob Grimm, co-publisher of *Grimm's Fairy Tales,* was born on this day in 1785. Write a summary of your favorite fairy tale.

The snowdrop is a flower that blooms in January. Pretend you are a famous botanist who has just discovered a very unusual plant that only blooms in January. Write about your discovery.

January 5

 George Washington Carver was born on January 5, 1864. He discovered over 300 uses for the peanut! Think of a brand-new product that is made from peanuts and write an advertisement describing your new product.

On this day in 1914 Henry Ford announced that all worthy Ford Motor Company employees would receive a minimum wage of $5 a day. Pretend you are a worker in Mr. Ford's plant during this time. Write him a letter asking for a raise.

January 6

American poet Carl Sandburg was born on this day in 1878. In honor of him, write a poem that has six lines. For an extra challenge, make each line have six words and make the last word in every line rhyme with *six!*

January's birthstone is a red gem known as a *garnet*. Imagine that a burglar has stolen the world's largest garnet from a national museum. Write a Wanted poster to help catch this cunning criminal!

January 7

George Washington won the first American presidential election on this day in 1789. Write a news article about the outcome of the first election as if it were going to be read by Americans on January 8, 1789.

Today marks the end of the first week of the new year. Look back on the past seven days and write a paragraph describing one thing that you'd do differently, and another thing that you'd do just the same.

January 8

Lyndon Johnson declared a war on poverty in his State of the Union address on this day in 1964. Imagine you've been given $1,000 to donate to the poor in your community. Whom would you give it to and how would you go about handing it out?

There are lots of special days set aside for all sorts of reasons—Secret Pal Day, Sandwich Day, and World Hello Day, just to name a few. Create a holiday of your own. What will it celebrate or honor? How will it be celebrated?

JANUARY

January 9

The month of January was named for *Janus,* the god of gates and doorways from Roman mythology. Janus had two faces that looked in opposite directions. How would your life change if you could see where you are going and where you have been at the same time?

What is your favorite sport? Write a convincing essay persuading the U.S. Congress to make your favorite sport the national sport.

January 10

January is National Hobby Month. Write about your favorite hobby, giving details about the hobby and telling how you got involved in it.

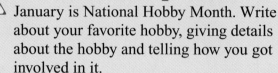Write down ten words that make a sound, like *buzz, pop,* or *bang.* Now think of a way to use all of the sound words you just listed in a short story.

January 11

Today is International Thank You Day. Write a thank-you note to someone who has done something special for you or your family.

Imagine that you've just gotten a really bad haircut. You are very embarrassed but realize that it may take weeks for your hair to grow back! Write a list of all the ways you could camouflage or cover up your head.

January 12

John Hancock, born on this day in 1737, was the first person to sign the Declaration of Independence. Many people call a signature a "John Hancock." What famous person's signature would you like to have as a souvenir? Explain why.

Pretend that you have a choice between a winter vacation in the mountains or a winter vacation at the beach. Make a list of *pros* (positives) and *cons* (negatives) about each location. Then write a paragraph explaining where you chose to go and why.

January 13

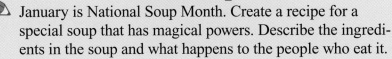

January is National Soup Month. Create a recipe for a special soup that has magical powers. Describe the ingredients in the soup and what happens to the people who eat it.

Homophones are words that sound the same but are spelled differently and have different meanings, such as *flour* and *flower*. Think of several pairs of homophones and use them in a funny story where the characters using the homophone pairs get them all mixed up.

January 14

Imagine that you wake up one weekend and it's too cold and wet to play outside. The power is also out, so there's no chance of watching TV, using the computer, or playing video games! How will you spend your day at home?

Once upon a time, believe it or not, your parents were the same age as you are! Write an imaginary diary entry that your mother or father might have written at your age.

January 15

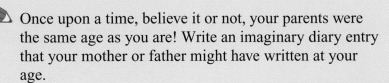

January 15, 1929, is the birthdate of Martin Luther King Jr., a civil rights leader and winner of the Nobel Peace Prize. He had a dream for the people of this country that included equality for all people, regardless of their race. If you had a dream, what would it be?

While eating your bowl of breakfast cereal one morning, something very strange starts to happen to you. Is it that you are shrinking, growing, turning blue, growing a tail, or...something else? Explain what happens and how you get back to normal.

January 16

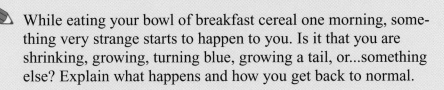

On this day in 1978, the United States National Aeronautics and Space Administration (NASA) accepted its first women candidates to become astronauts. Imagine that you have been accepted to become an astronaut. What are your thoughts, feelings, and goals in this exciting new career?

Pretend a spaceship lands in your backyard one day and the pilot invites you to go for a ride. Write all about your unusual adventure in space.

January 17

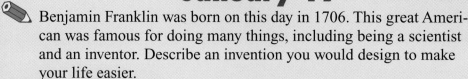

Benjamin Franklin was born on this day in 1706. This great American was famous for doing many things, including being a scientist and an inventor. Describe an invention you would design to make your life easier.

Ben Franklin was famous for his many sayings, such as, "Early to bed and early to rise, makes a man healthy, wealthy, and wise." Explain what you think Franklin meant by this quote. Come up with your own helpful piece of advice in the form of a saying. Explain what it means.

January 18

It's Pooh Day! Today honors the memory of A. A. Milne, the author of *Winnie the Pooh*, who was born on this day in January 1882. To celebrate this special occasion, write a letter to your favorite character from the Hundred Acre Wood.

Alliteration is the repetition of the same beginning sound in a series of words, such as, "The sleek, silvery sled slid speedily over the shimmering snow." Pick a letter to use as a beginning sound and write a sentence filled with alliteration.

January 19

Imagine that you are a writer for a successful advertising company. Write a catchy ad for a brand-new breakfast cereal.

Answer Your Cat's Question Day is observed in January. If your pet could talk, what do you think it would say to you?

Crispy Crunchers

Now CRISPIER

January 20

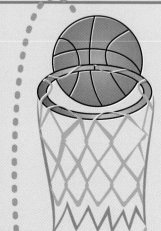

The first basketball game was played at a YMCA in Springfield, Massachusetts, on this day in 1892. To celebrate this event, pretend you are a player on your favorite NBA team. Write a short story about the time you sank the winning basket in the championship game!

Pets and other animals often need special care and attention during the winter months. Describe ways in which pet lovers can help animals keep warm and cozy during this chilly season.

January 21

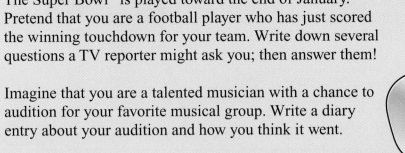

The Super Bowl® is played toward the end of January. Pretend that you are a football player who has just scored the winning touchdown for your team. Write down several questions a TV reporter might ask you; then answer them!

Imagine that you are a talented musician with a chance to audition for your favorite musical group. Write a diary entry about your audition and how you think it went.

January 22

Many people enjoy using the computer to surf the Internet. Describe what kinds of information and graphics you would put on a Web site of your very own.

Look at the January amounts of precipitation in the following locations: Seattle, Washington (5.4 inches); Rapid City, South Dakota (0.4 inches); Boston, Massachusetts (3.6 inches); and San Antonio, Texas (1.7 inches). Pretend you are a wacky weather reporter. Use this information to write a funny forecast for each of these cities.

January 23

Red? Green? Blue? Purple? Write down your favorite color, then make a list of all the things that are your favorite color. Now use this list to write a poem all about your favorite color.

What do Henry Barnard, John Holt, Horace Mann, Elizabeth Peabody, and Elizabeth Seton have in common? They were all famous educators! Write about one of your favorite teachers.

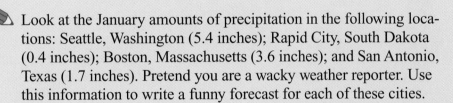

10 +13 23	11 + 8 19	7 +13 20
12 +13 25	10 + 3 13	9 +13 22

January 24

Many people enjoy creating types of art such as drawings, paintings, sculptures, and designs. What kind of art do you enjoy creating and why?

James W. Marshal accidentally discovered gold while building a sawmill near Coloma, California, on this day in 1848. Before long, his secret was out and the California gold rush was in full swing! Imagine that you've just discovered gold in your backyard. Write about whom you would trust with your very valuable secret and why.

January 25

 Transcontinental telephone service was set up in the United States on this day in 1915. Write an imaginary phone conversation between yourself and any person from the past or present that you would like to talk to.

Sometimes it's fun to get up at the crack of dawn before anyone else is awake. What do you like to do when you are the first one awake in your home?

January 26

 George F. Green patented the electric dental drill on this day in 1875. Write a make-believe letter to Mr. Green telling him what you think of his invention!

Today is Wayne Gretzky's birthday. To honor this famous hockey player, write a hockey story from the point of view of the hockey puck!

January 27

 Thomas Edison was given the first patent for the incandescent lightbulb on this day in 1880. Describe how this invention has made life easier for people all over the world.

 Pudding and Jell-O® are both refreshing treats. But what if they were the only two foods on earth? Make a list of all the different ways you could serve these two tasty treats that might make life with only two food choices a little less boring.

January 28

 Charles Schulz, Gary Larson, Stan Lee, Jim Davis—do you recognize these names? They are all famous cartoonists who have made many people smile all over the world. Describe a new cartoon character of your own creation and what makes him, her, or it special.

 Pretend that you are the last animal waiting to be bought in a pet store. Which animal would you be? Who will buy you? Write about your new home and whether you like it or not.

January 29

A cold winter day is a good time to curl up with a great book to read. What is one of your favorite books and why?

Many famous writers and entertainers change their names. Make a list of all the names that appeal to you. If you could choose a brand-new name, which one would it be and why would you choose this name?

January 30

Franklin D. Roosevelt was born on January 30, 1882. Roosevelt used a wheelchair after polio damaged his legs. He went on to be elected president of the United States four times, more than any other person. Write a success story where the main character overcomes a physical challenge.

Imagine that you've just found a bottle with a message inside. Write down what the message says and what you plan to do about it.

January 31

Imagine that you could design a dream house for your family. Describe the house you would design and list some of the special features that you would include to make your dream house special.

The *ptarmigan* is an Arctic bird that stays brown during the summer but turns white when snow covers the ground in winter. Write about what might happen if you could *camouflage,* or disguise, your body to match your surroundings just by thinking about it!

February 1

 February is American Heart Month. Describe an activity that you enjoy or a food that you eat that helps keep you healthy.

 Pretend that when you awoke this morning, you and your family found you had been transported to another country. Tell what country you're in and what you'll do next.

February 2

 Weather predictions from a groundhog? You bet! Today is Groundhog Day, and Punxsutawney Phil will emerge from his hole in the ground. If he sees his shadow, winter will last six more weeks. But if he doesn't, spring is just around the corner. Choose another animal that you think could do a good job of predicting the weather. Explain why.

You are a Secret Service agent, and your job is to guard the president. Describe a typical day.

February 3

 Has anyone ever told you, "I need eyes in the back of my head"? What do you think that means? Explain what life would be like if you really did have eyes in the back of your head.

The mail carrier has just delivered a package addressed to your parents. You can hear music coming from inside the box. Describe what's inside when the package is opened.

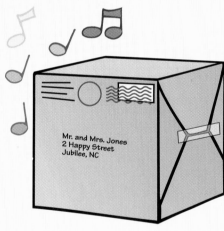

Mr. and Mrs. Jones
2 Happy Street
Jubilee, NC

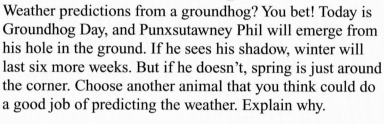

Hello, I am Glurk Bleep. I am 11 tangens old. I live on Zernon.

February 4

 Imagine what life would be like without computers. Describe a computer-free day.

 When you opened your email this morning, you had a message from someone who claimed to be from the planet Zernon. Write a response to the message.

February 5

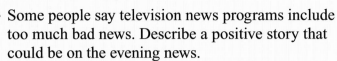

February is Black History Month. Think of a Black American whom you admire. Explain why.

Some people say television news programs include too much bad news. Describe a positive story that could be on the evening news.

February 6

When you washed your hair yesterday, something very unusual happened. Your shampoo made your hair turn green! Write a letter to the company explaining what happened. Include a description of how you and your family reacted.

Pretend that scientists have found a caveman who was frozen for 100,000 years. They have just unfrozen him and have asked *you* to explain to him what television, computers, and cars are. Tell how you would do this.

February 7

A magazine publisher has asked you to write a children's story about a princess who can turn into a superhero and save people in danger. Write an adventure for the princess.

The local newspaper suspects that the president of Big City Bank is stealing the bank's money. The editor has asked you to try to find out if this is true. What would you do?

February 8

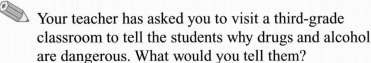

Congratulations! You have won the opportunity to direct a scene in a movie featuring your favorite celebrity. Whom would you choose? Describe the scene.

Your teacher has asked you to visit a third-grade classroom to tell the students why drugs and alcohol are dangerous. What would you tell them?

February 9

 Your neighbor's dog has just had puppies, and your parents said you could have one. Describe your first moments with the puppy.

 What do you think you will be doing on this day next year? Write a paragraph detailing your predictions.

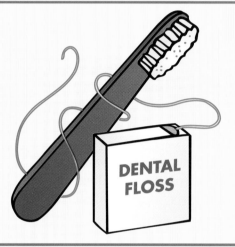

February 10

 February is National Children's Dental Health Month. Write a persuasive argument to convince a friend to brush and floss often.

 Imagine that today is February 10, 1820. You live in a log cabin. Describe what you will do today.

February 11

Have you ever heard the saying, "One person's trash is another person's treasure"? Have you ever found or been given an item that someone else was going to throw away? Describe it. Why did you like it?

February means the cold and flu season is upon us. What's the quickest way to help you feel better when you're sick? What's the quickest way to make you feel worse?

February 12

Today is President Abraham Lincoln's birthday! His nickname was Honest Abe. Write a paragraph telling why honesty is important.

You've lost your last baby tooth. You put it under your pillow and awaken to find that the Tooth Fairy has left you an unusual surprise. Describe your reaction.

February 13

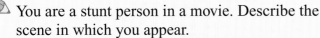

✏️ You are a stunt person in a movie. Describe the scene in which you appear.

✏️ Pretend that you have found an old love letter in your grandparents' basement. Whom is it from? To whom was it written? What does it say?

My dearest Clarence,

February 14

I think you are very special!

Shelly

✏️ It's Valentine's Day! Think of a famous person to whom you'd like to send a Valentine. Write your message.

✏️ Be an Encourager® Day is observed annually in February. Who has given you the most encouragement in your life? Explain your answer.

February 15

✏️ Imagine that one day you woke up and found that all the colors in the world had vanished. Fortunately you have a box of magic crayons that you can use to color the world in any way you want. Describe the colors you would use.

✏️ During summer hot spells, merchants often advertise cool drinks and other items to remind you of the frosty, blizzardy days of winter. What could you invent that would get everyone in the mood for a midwinter heat wave? Explain your invention.

February 16

✏️ You are exploring the Amazon and you discover a rare animal that could be of great use to humans. What is this animal? How can it help people?

✏️ Heart 2 Heart Day is observed annually two days after Valentine's Day. Write a heart-to-heart letter to someone who is extra special.

FEBRUARY

FEBRUARY

February 17

February is the birth month of baseball heroes Hank Aaron and Babe Ruth. Who do you think should be paid more: a teacher or a professional baseball player? Explain your answer.

Imagine that your house, school, playground, and community are underground. Describe a typical day.

February 18

Pretend that your parents have given you a video camera and you've decided to record your walk or ride to school. Describe what will be on your tape when you play it back.

Someday school may be completely different than it is today. For example, some people think that schools will use computers instead of books. Others think students will receive their assignments at home and won't even go to the school building. What changes do you predict?

February 19

Rrrrring! When you answer the telephone, you find that the person on the other end has dialed the wrong number. But he or she is in trouble and needs help. Explain what the problem is and how you can help.

The first American paper money was issued by Massachusetts in February 1690. If you had to name ten things that money *can't* buy, what would you list? Write your list in the order of importance to you, with number one being the most important item.

February 20

Describe the world through the eyes of your pet or a friend's pet.

Student Volunteer Day is observed on February 20. Make a list of all the ways you can volunteer in your school or community.

February 21

 February is Canned Food Month. Write down all the things that you've eaten in the past week that were packaged in a can.

 Choose a person who you think should be pictured on an American coin or dollar bill. Explain why the person should receive this honor.

February 22

 George "I-cannot-tell-a-lie" Washington was born on this day in 1732. If your best friend asked you an embarrassing question, would you tell the truth even if it was unpleasant or difficult to do so? Why or why not?

 You are taking a bath when a slimy green creature drops out of the faucet and into your bath water. Describe what happens next.

February 23

 You and your friend made a bet, and you lost. Now you have to do something silly on the street in front of your house. What would you do? How would you feel?

 Describe a time you cheered up someone who was hurt or sad.

February 24

Pretend that you have just received a mysterious package in the mail. The box contains $100 and a bag of your favorite candy. Who do you think sent the package? Why?

Imagine that Christopher Columbus didn't make his famous voyage in 1492. Instead, you are sailing with him today and he has just sighted land. Describe what happens next.

FEBRUARY

FEBRUARY

February 25

 National Pancake Week is observed each year in February. List as many toppings as you can think of for pancakes.

Pretend you are a bird that has flown south for the winter. Write a postcard to a fellow feathered friend who didn't fly south.

February 26

 As you were erasing a misspelled word in your journal, you made a startling discovery: If you rub the eraser on your skin, your skin disappears. What would you do next?

 Levi Strauss, the creator of the first pair of jeans, was born on this day in 1829. Describe your favorite outfit.

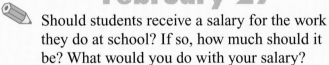

February 27

 Should students receive a salary for the work they do at school? If so, how much should it be? What would you do with your salary?

February is Snack Food Month. Write an expository paragraph telling how to make your favorite after-school snack.

February 28

 If you could invite a famous person to your birthday party, whom would it be? What would he or she do at the party?

 International Friendship Week is held during the last week of February. Write a recipe for the perfect friendship.

58

February 29

It's leap year! February has 29 days instead of 28. Pretend that February 29 is your birthday. Plan a special leap year birthday party for yourself.

Is there anything that you want so much that you would be willing to save all of your own money to get it? Explain your answer.

Come to Jeremy's Leap Year Birthday Party!

MARCH

March 1

 On March 1, 1872, the area in Wyoming, Montana, and Idaho known as Yellowstone became the world's first national park. Celebrate this occasion by choosing one of our national parks to use as a setting for an outdoor adventure story.

Oink, oink! Today is National Pig Day! Remember Wilbur, Babe, and many other pigs who have starred in stories you have read or movies you have seen? Honor all pigs in a poem or essay for this special day.

March 2

 Celebrated on Dr. Seuss's birthday, today has been designated Read Across America Day. To honor the birth of this talented children's book writer, compose a ridiculous rhyming poem.

Remember the first time you read *Green Eggs and Ham*? Create an entire menu of unusual foods to be served at a birthday feast in Dr. Seuss's honor.

March 3

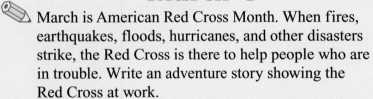

 March is American Red Cross Month. When fires, earthquakes, floods, hurricanes, and other disasters strike, the Red Cross is there to help people who are in trouble. Write an adventure story showing the Red Cross at work.

The Star-Spangled Banner was adopted as our national anthem on March 3, 1931. Write a poem or song of your own about our country.

March 4

March is National Women's History Month, a time to celebrate the many ways in which women have contributed to American history. Choose one woman from the past or present that you admire and write why you think so much of her.

What if you had an invisible friend? Write a funny story about the day your invisible friend decides to follow you to school!

March 5

To celebrate National Umbrella Month, imagine that you have just invented an incredible umbrella that has unusual uses or powers. Write a lively advertisement describing this new and improved umbrella!

There's an old saying that goes "March comes in like a lion and goes out like a lamb." Explain what you think this means; then find two new animals to use for this saying and explain why you chose them.

March 6

March 6, 1475, is the birthday of the famous painter and poet, Michelangelo. Make a list of other famous people that are known by only one name; then give them last names that reveal something about their fame. Choose several people on your list and explain why you chose the last name for them that you did.

In honor of Youth Art Month, imagine that you have created a fantastic work of art which is going to be displayed in a local art gallery. Write the description that would be displayed next to your work of art.

March 7

The Monopoly® game was invented on March 7, 1933. Pretend that you are talking to someone who has never played a board game before. Write down the directions for how this game is played. Be careful! Don't leave out any steps!

Imagine that you are playing a new board game with a friend, and you discover that whatever happens in the game starts to happen in real life! Describe the game and your experiences while playing it.

Mon.	Tues.	Wed.	Thurs.	Fri.	Sat.	Sun.	?

March 8

March is Optimism Month, a time to accentuate the positive. Write about a time when looking on the bright side has helped you through a tough experience.

What if every week had eight days instead of seven? What would you call this eighth day of the week and how would you spend it?

March 9

 More than 800 million Barbie® dolls have been sold since her first appearance on March 9, 1959! Write about a popular toy that you have enjoyed owning or create a brand-new toy that you'd like to see sold in stores.

 Pretend that you could have a conversation with one of your favorite toys. Which toy would it be and what would you talk about? Write out the dialogue.

March 10

 Harriet Tubman died on March 10, 1913. This famous woman was born a slave in 1821 and eventually led over 300 slaves to freedom. Write a thank-you letter to this brave woman for choosing to risk her life in order to save the lives of so many others.

 What does it mean to be brave? Write about a time when you or someone you know acted bravely.

March 11

 Johnny Appleseed Day is celebrated on the anniversary of John Chapman's death, March 11, 1845. Chapman was known for planting apple orchards throughout the frontier of Ohio and Indiana. Write about the many ways in which apples are useful to people.

 Imagine that you are one of the apples hanging on an apple tree at harvest time. A family carrying a basket approaches your tree. Write about what happens from your point of view.

March 12

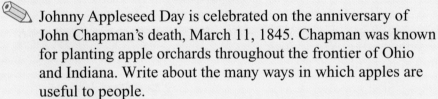 Juliet Low founded the Girl Scouts of the USA on March 12, 1912. More than 2½ million girls belong to the Girl Scouts of the USA. Do you belong to a club? Write about the club you belong to or would like to belong to. What makes this club special to you?

 Recess is a favorite time of day for many students. Write a letter to your principal trying to convince him or her to add more time to your recess period! Remember to include specific points to back up your argument.

M A R C H

March 13

 Uranus, the seventh planet from the Sun, was discovered on March 13, 1781. Pretend you've just discovered the tenth planet! Describe this new planet. Does it contain life forms? If so, what do they look like?

National Agriculture Week is celebrated in March, during the week that includes the first day of spring. Think about all the farmers who work very hard to provide food for this country. Write a letter of thanks to the many farmers of America.

March 14

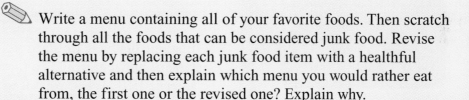 Children and Healthcare Week™ takes place during March. To celebrate, write an *acrostic poem* (a poem that can be read both down and across). Use each letter in the word *health* to begin a new line of your poem.

Write a menu containing all of your favorite foods. Then scratch through all the foods that can be considered junk food. Revise the menu by replacing each junk food item with a healthful alternative and then explain which menu you would rather eat from, the first one or the revised one? Explain why.

March 15

 What makes you happy? Make a list of things that make you happy and choose three to write about in more detail.

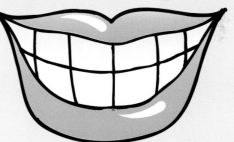

Pretend that you are holding a covered box that is seven inches long, four inches wide, and three inches high. There is something inside the box. Describe what it is by using sensory details, such as how it smells, how it feels, and how it sounds.

March 16

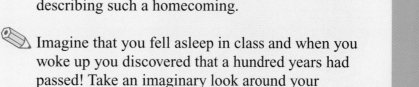 Many birds that migrate to warmer climates during winter return to their natural habitats during March. Write a diary entry from a bird's point of view describing such a homecoming.

Imagine that you fell asleep in class and when you woke up you discovered that a hundred years had passed! Take an imaginary look around your futuristic classroom and describe what you see.

March 17

It's fun to pretend you are Irish on St. Patrick's Day, the day many people honor the patron saint of Ireland. Think about shamrocks, leprechauns, and pots of gold. Then put them all together with a little creative magic to write a fun holiday story.

As spring approaches, many things in nature start to turn green once again. Imagine that you woke up one morning only to discover that *you* had turned green overnight! Write about your day and how you finally returned to your normal color!

March 18

Each spring, the Academy of Motion Picture Arts and Sciences presents awards, called *Oscar Awards®,* to the best actor, director, and movie, etc., from the previous year. Write a movie review about a film from the previous year that you think deserves an Oscar®.

Imagine that you are starring in a movie! Describe the type of movie it would be (action, adventure, fantasy, science fiction) and what it would be about.

March 19

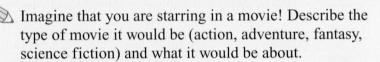

March is Music in Our Schools Month. Write about the music program in your school and what it means to you.

Imagine that you are listening to the radio one afternoon when the disc jockey announces that the next song is dedicated to you! Write a short mystery describing the clues that help you find out who dedicated the song to you.

March 20

Spring begins in the Northern Hemisphere on March 20 or 21. Write a spring poem or essay describing your feelings about this season of rebirth and renewal.

Maple sap is tapped at this time of year and made into maple sugar and maple syrup. Pretend you are a food critic and write a review of a restaurant called "The Maple Syrup Shack."

March 21

March is not only the name of a month, it is also a verb that means "walking with a regular step." People often join together to march for a special cause, such as muscular dystrophy or racial equality, in order to bring attention to that cause. Name one special cause that you would be willing to march for and explain why.

Have you ever listened to two birds chirping in the trees and wondered what they were saying to each other? Make believe you could actually understand their language for one magical morning. Write down what the two birds said to each other word for word.

March 22

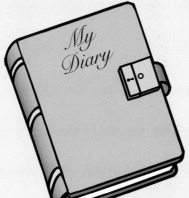

National Clutter Awareness Week is observed annually the last full week in March. Write about all the unusual, interesting, or funny things you might find while cleaning out your room.

While helping your parents clean out the attic, you come across an old trunk. Inside is a diary from one of your great-great-grandparents! Write down what you read on one of the diary pages.

March 23

On March 23, 1989, a mountain-sized asteroid passed within 500,000 miles of Earth, a very close call according to NASA. Describe a near miss you may have recently experienced.

Imagine that you come home from school one day and find a large wrapped package on the kitchen table. It has your name on the label with no return name or address. You quickly open it and gasp in surprise! Describe what is in the package, who it is from, and what effect this unexpected gift will have on you.

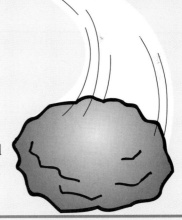

March 24

On March 24, 1989, the tanker *Exxon Valdez* ran aground off the shore of Alaska and leaked 11 million gallons of oil into Prince William Sound, one of nature's richest habitats. Write a newspaper account about the effects of this disaster.

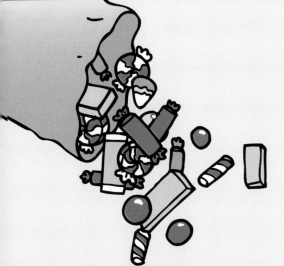

If you worked for a candy company, what new candy would you invent? What would it taste and look like? How would you package it and what would you call it?

March 25

 On this day in 1775, George Washington planted several pecan trees (some of which still survive) at Mount Vernon. The trees were a gift from Thomas Jefferson, who had already planted a few pecan trees from the southern United States at Monticello, Virginia. Write a thank-you card from George Washington to Thomas Jefferson in appreciation of this nutty gift.

Think of two colors. Now think of something that has those two colors on it. Is it a person, an animal, a place, or a thing? Describe what it looks like and any other details that you think might help someone guess what it is you are describing.

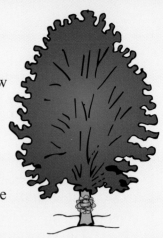

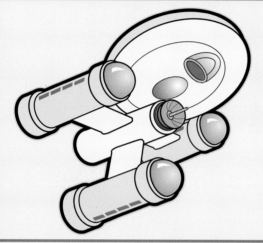

March 26

 Today is Leonard Nimoy's birthday. In honor of this talented actor who played Spock in dozens of *Star Trek* episodes and several *Star Trek* movies, write a short science fiction story that boldly takes your readers "...where no man has gone before."

March is usually considered a windy month. Write a funny story or poem about a windy day.

March 27

On this day in 1964, the strongest earthquake in North American history struck Alaska, recording 8.4 on the Richter scale! Pretend you were an eyewitness to this historic event and write a brief account of what you saw, felt, and heard that day.

Remember the first time you heard the fairy tale *Goldilocks and the Three Bears*? Rewrite the classic story by telling it from Baby Bear's point of view.

TIK-A
TIK-A

March 28

Over 800,000 species of insects have been discovered so far! Imagine that you are an *entomologist,* an insect scientist, who has discovered a brand-new insect. Describe the insect and where it was discovered; then give the creepy-crawly a name.

 Imagine that the United States government wants to print a new bill worth $15.00. What famous person's face do you think should be on this new bill? Write a convincing letter to the president explaining your choice.

March 29

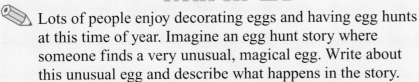 Lots of people enjoy decorating eggs and having egg hunts at this time of year. Imagine an egg hunt story where someone finds a very unusual, magical egg. Write about this unusual egg and describe what happens in the story.

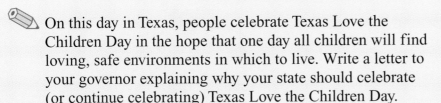 On this day in Texas, people celebrate Texas Love the Children Day in the hope that one day all children will find loving, safe environments in which to live. Write a letter to your governor explaining why your state should celebrate (or continue celebrating) Texas Love the Children Day.

March 30

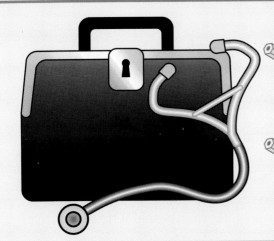 Since 1933, March 30 has honored our country's doctors with Doctors' Day. Write a poem or paragraph about a doctor who has made a positive impression on you.

March 30, 1858, marks the date when the first pencil with the eraser top was patented by Hyman Lipman. Pretend the pencil and the pen had never been invented, and describe what life would be like without these two valuable writing utensils.

March 31

 This is the last day of March. Look back over the past month and write about your favorite memories from March. If you could do one thing differently, what would it be and why?

People often place bumper stickers with special messages on their cars' bumpers. Create your own positive bumper sticker slogan. Write about the slogan and explain its purpose and meaning.

HAVE YOU HUGGED YOUR TEACHER TODAY?

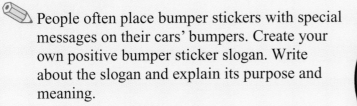

M A R C H

April 1

April Fools' Day is observed on April 1. Write about the best joke you ever played on someone.

April is Keep America Beautiful Month. Describe the most beautiful place in your neighborhood, town, or city.

April 2

In many parts of the country the snow has already melted. Imagine that you are the very last snowflake of the season. Explain how you have survived this long, how you feel, and what you plan to do now that winter's finally over.

Juan Ponce de Leon discovered Florida on this day in 1513. Florida is known as the Sunshine State because of its beautiful weather and sunny climate. If you could think of a new nickname for your state, what would it be and why?

April 3

Imagine that two eggs in your Easter basket are having a conversation. Write what they are saying to each other.

Springtime can be blustery! Imagine that you're walking down the street when the wind blows your hat into a dark alley. Write about what you find when you chase your hat down the alley.

That's an "eggs-cellent" idea!

April 4

Many animals have their babies in the spring. Think of your favorite baby animal. Now write a story or poem describing how the baby changes as it matures.

Pretend you have just opened the refrigerator and taken out a carton of eggs. Suddenly one of the eggs starts to crack. Something is hatching! Describe what happens next.

April 5

 April is National Garden Month. If you had your own garden, what kinds of plants or vegetables would you be sure *not* to plant? Explain why.

 Imagine that you are outside blowing bubbles with your best friend. You blow a really big bubble—so big that it surrounds the two of you and begins to carry you away. Tell what happens next.

April 6

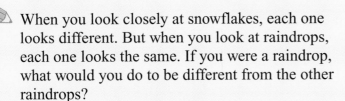

 Warm spring days are perfect for picnics. Pretend that you are an ant that has crawled into an open picnic basket. Describe the picnic from the ant's point of view.

Imagine that you are a seed sprouting. Describe how it feels to spread your roots, emerge from the dirt, and bloom.

April 7

 Bunnies and chicks symbolize Easter for many people. If you had to choose a different animal to represent Easter, what animal would you choose? Explain your reasons.

When you look closely at snowflakes, each one looks different. But when you look at raindrops, each one looks the same. If you were a raindrop, what would you do to be different from the other raindrops?

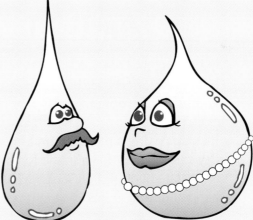

April 8

 Pretend that you are a kite. Your string has broken and you can float anywhere in the world. Write a story telling about your adventures.

If you could fill a basket with your favorite things, what would your basket contain? List five items and explain what they mean to you.

APRIL

April 9

April is known for its blustery winds. Imagine that you are the wind. Are you a strong wind or a gentle breeze? A raging tornado or the calm before the storm? Write about what type of wind you are and why.

World Health Day is observed in April each year. Write one thing you could do to become a healthier person. Then write a plan for how you can accomplish it.

10 Great Reasons to Visit Broomtown

April 10

During spring cleaning your parents insist that you clean out your closet. When you reach way in the back, you find a locked box that you've never seen before. Write about how you open it and what you find inside.

You have been put in charge of an advertising campaign to bring tourists to your town on vacation. Create a travel brochure that tells what your town has to offer and why people should visit it.

April 11

Your parents have decided to redecorate the house, and you are allowed to choose how to decorate your bedroom. How would you like your room to look?

Instead of drops of water, imagine that one day rain poured down in the form of chocolate pudding! Describe what would happen during a "pudding storm."

April 12

April is National Humor Month. What is the funniest book you have ever read? What was so funny about it?

During a stroll in the park, you see a frog sitting on a park bench. Instead of hopping away when you sit down beside him, this frog strikes up a conversation with you. Write about what happens when the two of you begin talking.

70

April 13

To celebrate spring, plan a Frisbee® competition for your school. What events will the contest include? How will contestants win? What will be the grand prize?

What sounds do you usually hear outside your bedroom window in the morning? Imagine that one morning you hear something completely different. Describe what you hear.

2 points

April 14

As you are taking a walk one afternoon, you find a hidden fountain. A sign says that if you drink from this fountain you will stay the same age forever. Would you take a drink? Describe what you would do and why.

The ocean liner *Titanic* struck an iceberg on this day in 1912, causing it to sink. Pretend you are a deep-sea diver who is exploring the ship's wreckage. What sunken treasures do you find?

April 15

April is National Poetry Month. Write a poem about spring.

Leonardo da Vinci, an Italian artist and inventor, was born on this day in 1452. Da Vinci often wrote backwards in his notebooks. Describe a backwards day. Plan a schedule for the day, in which you do things from the end to the beginning.

Today's Schedule

7:00 AM Dinner—fried chicken

7:30 AM Walk backwards to school

8:00 AM Read book starting with "The End"

April 16

Show me the money! Write a persuasive letter to your parents explaining why you should get an allowance, how much it should be, and why this amount of money is so reasonable.

Zoom! An insect unlike any you've ever seen before has just flown by you. Describe this new bug. What makes it different from other bugs you've seen before?

April 17

When you woke up this morning, you weren't yourself—literally! Instead, you were your teacher, principal, mother, father, or some other adult. Describe who you are and what your day is like.

Describe the first time you rode your bike without training wheels. How did you feel? Who was there? How did they react?

April 18

Write a descriptive paragraph about your favorite springtime flower.

National Volunteer Week is in April. Write a paragraph explaining the importance of volunteers in your school.

April 19

Spring is a time when many flowers bloom. But what if someone replaced your flower seeds with candy? Describe what kind of fanciful flowers might grow in your imaginary candy garden.

Pie is the favorite dessert of many people. If you could write a recipe for a new kind of pie, what flavor would it be? What ingredients would you need?

April 20

The last full week in April is Professional Secretaries Week. Write a letter to your school secretary thanking her for all of the things she does to keep your school running so smoothly.

With so many plants growing in the spring there are lots of chores to do, such as mowing grass, weeding flower beds, and planting vegetables. Describe a new invention that would make performing these chores easier.

April 21

Are you ready for a day off from school? Congratulations! You are now in charge of creating a new spring holiday! Name your holiday and describe how to celebrate it. Then explain why students should have this day off school.

Bike riding is fun, but sometimes it can also be dangerous. Design a super safe bicycle that would eliminate some of the danger. Describe what it looks like and why it is safer than other bikes.

April 22

Today is Earth Day. Imagine that you are in charge of an Earth Day celebration for your school. What events would you plan?

Have you ever heard the saying, "You can't fool Mother Nature"? Pretend that you once tried to fool Mother Nature. Describe what happened.

April 23

The tallest man in medical history was about nine feet tall. Imagine that you have grown even taller! Describe what your typical day would be like.

On this day in 1949, Governor Adlai E. Stevenson of Illinois vetoed a bill that would require cats to be leashed. Governor Stevenson believed it to be a cat's nature to roam independently. Do you agree? List five things a pet owner can do to ensure his pet isn't a nuisance to others.

April 24

Today is National Puppetry Day! Celebrate by creating an original puppet; then write a short puppet show in which your new character is the star.

The average housefly lives only two weeks. If you were a fly in your house, describe how you would spend that short amount of time.

APRIL

APRIL

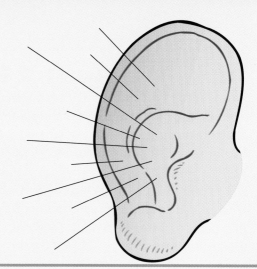

April 25

 Imagine that you have just made a fantastic discovery. Now it's time to announce it to the world! Describe what the discovery is and why it's so exciting. Explain how others react to your announcement.

April is Listening Awareness Month. Describe a time when you wish you had listened better than you did.

April 26

 How would you spend the perfect day? What would you do? Where would you go? Describe your day.

 Pretend that a famous artist has come to draw your portrait. In the background of the picture, the artist would like to show items that symbolize your interests and hobbies. What would these items be and why?

April 27

 Today marks the beginning of National Playground Safety Week. Celebrate by designing the safest playground in town. Then write a grand opening announcement describing why your playground is so safe.

Imagine that you have a packet of magic seeds. What might happen when you plant them?

SUPER-DUPER
MAGIC SEEDS

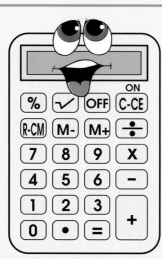

April 28

 Has anyone ever said to you, "You're just like your mother," or, "Your grandpa used to do that same thing"? Describe a physical trait, mannerism, or attitude that makes you similar to another family member.

 April is Mathematics Education Month. Make a list of all the ways you use math in your life.

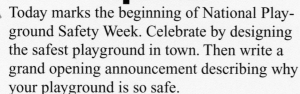

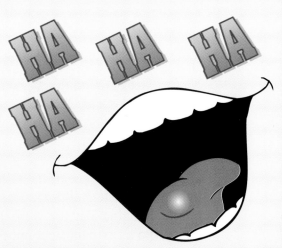

April 29

Today is Moment of Laughter Day. In honor of this hilarious occasion, write a funny short story or poem that might make people laugh.

Ready for a nice spring picnic? Describe what you'll pack in your picnic basket and where you'll go.

April 30

National Arbor Day is held on the last Friday in April. Did you know that recycling just one four-foot stack of newspapers saves a 35- to 40-foot tree? Celebrate this "tree-mendous" holiday by making a list of all the ways you can conserve paper in the classroom.

Congratulations! The Up, Up, and Away Kite Design Contest has just announced that you are its grand-prize winner! Describe your kite and all of the special features that set it apart from the other contestants.

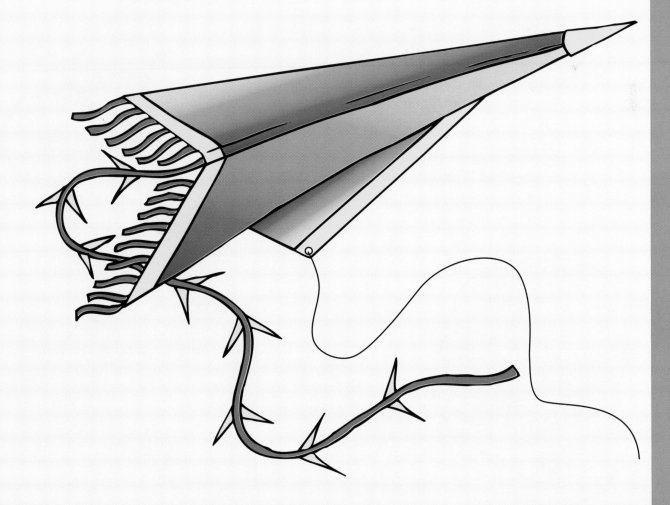

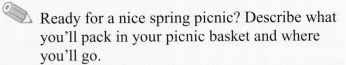

APRIL

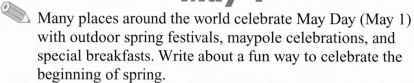

May 1

 Many places around the world celebrate May Day (May 1) with outdoor spring festivals, maypole celebrations, and special breakfasts. Write about a fun way to celebrate the beginning of spring.

 On May 1, 1931, one of the tallest buildings in the world, the Empire State Building, was finally opened to the public. Imagine that you were the first guest allowed to the top. Write a firsthand account of what you saw that day.

May 2

 Be Kind to Animals Week® takes place during the first full week of May. Pretend you are an animal, such as a dog or a cat, and write about several ways that humans can be kind to you and your fellow animal friends.

 The emerald is the birthstone for May. Imagine that you found an expensive emerald ring while walking through the park. Describe in detail the steps you will take to find the ring's owner and whether or not you will ask for a reward.

May 3

 May is National Bike Month. Write a list of all the ways you can make riding your bike a safe, fun activity.

 Your bike has been stolen! Write and solve a short mystery titled "The Case of the Missing Bike."

May 4

 National Hamburger Month is observed during the month of May. Create a tasty but unusual new hamburger and list all of its ingredients and toppings. Then name your burger and write a brief menu description for your creation.

 If you had 20 square feet of land to make your very own garden and could plant anything you wanted to, what would you plant and why?

May 5

🖊 S-t-r-e-t-c-h and yawn! May is Better Sleep Month. Imagine that your friend has *insomnia,* or trouble sleeping. Describe some interesting ways to help your friend get to sleep.

🖊 Congratulations! You've just been given the job of waking up your family of heavy sleepers every single morning. Write about some creative methods you can use to get your family out of bed.

May 6

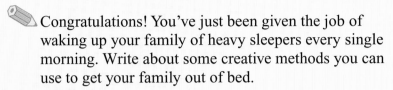

 In honor of National Salad Month, create an unusual new salad that has at least eight different ingredients. List the ingredients; then explain in a paragraph why you chose each ingredient for your salad.

 Pretend that you are a famous scientist who has just discovered a cure for one of the world's deadliest diseases. Describe your discovery and its impact on the world.

May 7

🖊 May is Older Americans Month. Write a poem in honor of an older American that you know and respect.

🖊 Imagine that you woke up one morning only to find that you were suddenly 80 years old! Write one diary entry from the day before, when you were still a kid, and another describing how different your day would be at your new age.

May 8

 On May 8, 1914, the U.S. Congress and the president officially declared that the second Sunday in May would be set aside to honor all mothers. Write a poem or essay honoring your mother or a person who has been just like a mother to you.

 Make a list of some of the special times or events you've experienced in your life. Then pick one of the events to describe in detail.

La, la, la, I can't hear you...

May 9

 Remember all the stories you have read about animal mothers and their babies? Compose a greeting card from one such animal baby to its mother.

 May is Better Hearing Month. Describe in detail three things you are most likely to "tune out" and not hear.

PLEASE

THANK YOU

May 10

 National Etiquette Week is the second week of May. Make a list of all the ways you can think of to show off your good manners when speaking, eating, and being around other people. Then use your list to help you write a paragraph about using good manners.

 "Please" and "thank you" can be magical words. Write an imaginative story where every time those words are used properly, something wonderful happens to the person who says them.

May 11

 A number of birds are patiently sitting on eggs in nests at this time of year. Write about something you do that requires you to be very patient.

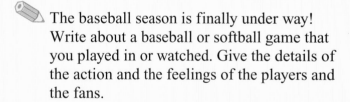 The baseball season is finally under way! Write about a baseball or softball game that you played in or watched. Give the details of the action and the feelings of the players and the fans.

May 12

 Florence Nightingale, the founder of modern nursing, was born on this day in 1820. Write a short rescue story where a nurse is the heroine.

 Edward Lear was born on May 12, 1812. He was the poet who invented limericks. A limerick is a five-line poem with lines 1, 2, and 5 rhyming. Lines 3 and 4 may or may not rhyme. Now that you know what a limerick is, try writing one!

May 13

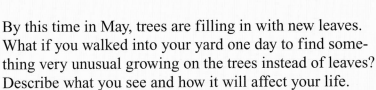

Many people consider the number thirteen to be unlucky. Why not make thirteen a lucky number? Make a list of thirteen ways in which you feel you are a lucky person.

By this time in May, trees are filling in with new leaves. What if you walked into your yard one day to find something very unusual growing on the trees instead of leaves? Describe what you see and how it will affect your life.

May 14

Meriwether Lewis and William Clark left St. Louis on this date in the year 1804, in search of a route to the Pacific Ocean. They succeeded in 1805 by arriving at Oregon's Pacific coast. List several places in the world you would like to explore and choose one to write about in detail.

You've just invited the new student from school over to your house to play. But she doesn't know your town very well. Write the exact directions this student will need to follow to get from the school to your house.

May 15

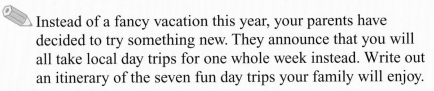

L. Frank Baum, the author of *The Wonderful Wizard of Oz,* was born on May 15, 1856. Pretend those glittery ruby slippers didn't work. Write a diary entry Dorothy might write if she still lived in Oz after all of these years.

Instead of a fancy vacation this year, your parents have decided to try something new. They announce that you will all take local day trips for one whole week instead. Write out an itinerary of the seven fun day trips your family will enjoy.

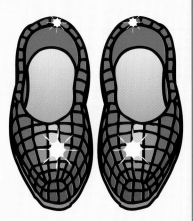

May 16

On this day in 1866, the United States authorized the first nickel. What do you think you could buy for five cents back in 1866? What can you buy for a nickel today?

While looking for something in the basement of your house, you come across a hidden door that you have never seen before. You pull the door open on its rusty hinges and...then what? Write a story about what happens next!

May 17

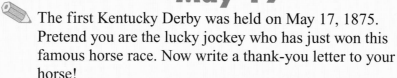
The first Kentucky Derby was held on May 17, 1875. Pretend you are the lucky jockey who has just won this famous horse race. Now write a thank-you letter to your horse!

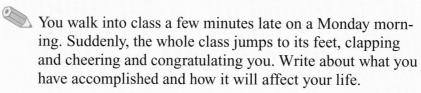
You walk into class a few minutes late on a Monday morning. Suddenly, the whole class jumps to its feet, clapping and cheering and congratulating you. Write about what you have accomplished and how it will affect your life.

May 18

Mount St. Helens, a volcano in Washington state, erupted on May 18, 1980. Imagine you were sightseeing a few miles from the volcano on that day and saw it all happen. Describe what you saw in a riveting eyewitness account.

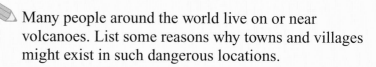
Many people around the world live on or near volcanoes. List some reasons why towns and villages might exist in such dangerous locations.

May 19

You and your friends have decided to prepare and deliver special May baskets to people in need. What will you put in such a May basket and whom will you give it to?

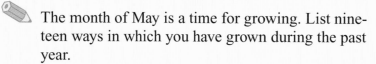
The month of May is a time for growing. List nineteen ways in which you have grown during the past year.

May 20

On May 20, 1862, President Lincoln signed the Homestead Act. This provided millions of acres of government-owned land in the West for settlers, or *homesteaders,* to live on and cultivate for five years. If you could live anywhere in the world for five years, where would it be and why?

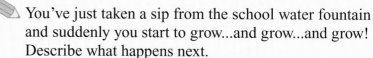
You've just taken a sip from the school water fountain and suddenly you start to grow...and grow...and grow! Describe what happens next.

May 21

On this date in 1927, Charles Lindbergh became the first person to fly solo across the Atlantic Ocean. He flew from New York to Paris in 33$\frac{1}{2}$ hours. Pretend you are Lindbergh and record your thoughts during the last half hour of this historic flight.

There have been lots of people who have been the first to accomplish something that had never been done before. What future event would you like to be the first to accomplish?

May 22

This week is International Pickle Week. List all of the different words (real or made-up) that could possibly rhyme with *pickles*. Now write a humorous poem in honor of pickles.

To be "in a pickle" means to be in a difficult situation, to be stuck, or to have some kind of a problem. Write about a time when you were in a pickle. Explain the situation and how you got out of this pickle.

May 23

On May 23, 1975, Junko Tabei, a Japanese housewife, became the first woman to reach the top of Mount Everest, the world's tallest mountain. Sir Edmund Hillary and Sherpa Tenzing Norgay were the first men to accomplish this same feat in 1953. Describe the skills and attitude you think are necessary to climb such a mountain. Tell why you think these brave people risked the climb.

You have decided to join a team of mountain climbers who are going to try to reach the top of Mount McKinley, the tallest mountain in North America. Describe your adventure in the form of a phone call home to your worried parents.

May 24

In an effort to promote healthy lungs, the American Lung Association has named May Breathe Easy Month. One way to have healthy lungs is by not smoking. Write a thank-you letter from a pair of lungs to someone who has just quit smoking.

Some states have laws banning smoking in public places. Give your opinion of these laws and explain your point of view.

May 25

George Herman Ruth, better known as "Babe" to his many fans, was born on this day in 1895. Babe Ruth was a great baseball slugger who went on to knock an amazing 714 home runs out of the park! Write a fan letter to your favorite athlete, famous or not.

As the weather gets warmer, people start to dress differently. Write an article for a fashion magazine describing the change of fashions for this spring season.

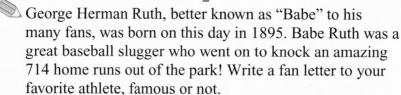

May 26

This is a popular time of year for garage sales and yard sales. Imagine that you've just discovered that something you bought at a yard sale is actually a very valuable antique! Write a list of the pros and cons of keeping the item and a list of the pros and cons of selling the item.

A person your age has just moved in next door to you. What advice or help can you offer your new neighbor to help him or her get adjusted to the neighborhood?

May 27

On this date in 1930, R. G. Drew got the first patent for adhesive cellophane tape. Write an advertisement that might have appeared describing all the wonderful uses for this new tape.

The National Spelling Bee Finals in Washington, DC, are held each year at the end of May. Imagine that you are the finalist representing your state at the spelling bee and have just been given an exceptionally hard word to spell. Describe your feelings and whether or not you spell the word correctly.

May 28

May is National Physical Fitness and Sports Month. Are you physically fit? Write an honest evaluation of your own level of physical fitness and what you can do to maintain or improve it.

Spring is a great season for playing games and sports outdoors. Select one game or sport that you enjoy and describe in detail how it is played.

May 29

Wisconsin became the 30th state on this day in 1848. If you could create the 51st state anywhere in the world, where would it be and why?

Each state has its very own license plate. Some license plates are rather plain and some have colorful designs or pictures on them. Write a review of your state's license plate and make several suggestions for a brand-new design.

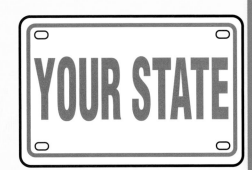

YOUR STATE

May 30

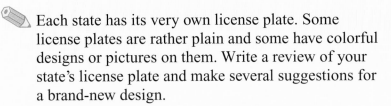

On May 30, 1783, *The Pennsylvania Evening Post* became the first daily newspaper published in the United States. If you could create a newspaper just for kids, what would you call it and what kinds of stories would fill its pages?

Lots of people enjoy fishing at this time of year. Sometimes the stories fishermen tell about "the fish that got away" can be slightly exaggerated. Make up a larger-than-life fish tale of your own.

May 31

Celebrated on this day, Memorial Day honors the memory of the brave Americans who died while serving the United States in war. Write a poem or paragraph to honor these special people.

Many cities organize big parades to celebrate Memorial Day. If you were in charge of decorating your school's float for a parade, what would it look like and who would ride on it?

 MAY

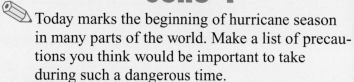

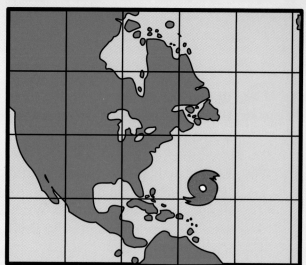

June 1

Today marks the beginning of hurricane season in many parts of the world. Make a list of precautions you think would be important to take during such a dangerous time.

Most schools are closed for several months during the summer. Describe several ways in which school buildings could be used to benefit your community during these summer months.

June 2

The first full week of June is National Fishing Week. Write a diary entry about this occasion from a fish's point of view!

You are in charge of designing a new summer camp for kids. What is the focus or purpose of the camp? Describe a typical day at camp.

June 3

June Dairy Month is a time for honoring the contributions of America's dairy farmers. List ten dairy products; then write a paragraph explaining the importance of dairy products in your diet.

Many schools are closing for the summer during the first week of June. Describe how your life would be different if school was let out at some other time of year.

June 4

When Michael Kearney was only ten years old, he graduated from the University of South Alabama. Write a graduation speech that a ten-year-old might make.

Summer months mean summer chores! Write a story titled "The Runaway Vacuum."

June 5

✏️ The school year is drawing to an end. As you reflect on it, what was the highlight of your year?

✏️ If you found a magic skateboard, where would you ride it to and what would you do when you got there?

June 6

✏️ National Fragrance Week is celebrated the first full week in June. If you were blindfolded, what smells would let you know that you were at school and not someplace else?

✏️ Your parents have put you in charge of setting up the backyard with a sprinkler system to entertain the neighborhood kids on a hot day. Describe what kind of sprinklers and water toys you provide. Be creative.

June 7

✏️ Some year-round schools are still in session during the month of June. Are you in favor of year-round schools? Write an argument for or against such a schedule.

✏️ If you were at a mall and found a bag with $500 in it, what would you do? Explain your decision.

June 8

✏️ June is Fireworks Safety Month. Make a list of safety tips you think should be included on the back of every package of fireworks.

✏️ Many people enjoy taking summertime rides in hot-air balloons. Write about what would happen if you climbed into the basket of a hot-air balloon and the wind carried you far, far away.

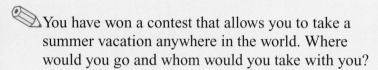

June 9

The cartoon character Donald Duck® was "born" on June 9. If ducks could really talk, what would they say? Write a conversation between two ducks who might be jealous of Donald Duck's fame.

You have won a contest that allows you to take a summer vacation anywhere in the world. Where would you go and whom would you take with you?

June 10

June is National Pest Control Month. Have you ever been a *pest*? Explain.

Create a brand-new ride for an amusement park. Give it a clever name and describe what the ride does and how the ride makes a person feel.

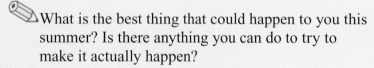

June 11

Today is the birthday of Jacques Cousteau, the great undersea explorer. If you could explore the ocean depths, what new creature would you like to discover? Describe it.

What is the best thing that could happen to you this summer? Is there anything you can do to try to make it actually happen?

June 12

The National Safety Council has designated June National Safety Month. Celebrate by naming ten different ways you can make your life safer each and every day.

What is the worst thing that could happen to you this summer? How likely is it to happen? What could you do to avoid it?

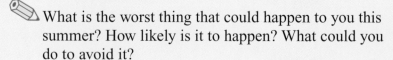

June 13

✏️ Today marks the beginning of National Hermit Week. Write a paragraph debating the pros and cons of living all alone.

✏️ Pretend you are a sandal on the foot of your favorite movie star. Describe where you go and what your average day is like.

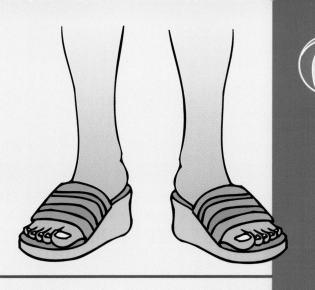

June 14

✏️ In honor of Flag Day, design a special flag for your school, club, or family. Explain why each part of the flag was chosen and what it represents.

✏️ While reading a story that takes place 100 years ago, one of the characters steps out of the book and into your room. Explain what happens next.

June 15

✏️ June is Vision Research Month. Pretend you have just invented a pair of X-ray glasses; then write an advertisement enticing people to buy them.

✏️ More s'mores! Marshmallows, chocolate, and graham crackers make an easy camping dessert. Write about another tasty treat that is just as easy to make.

June 16

✏️ While on vacation at the beach, you enter a sand castle contest and win! Write a short story about the miniature royal family that moves into your prizewinning sand castle.

✏️ Imagine that you are a grain of sand lying on the beach. Describe what happens to you when a huge wave sweeps you into the ocean and tries to suck you out to sea.

JUNE

June 17

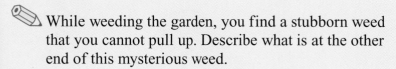
June has been named National Iced Tea Month in honor of this drink's refreshing nature. Celebrate by writing about a time when a thirst-quenching drink made your day.

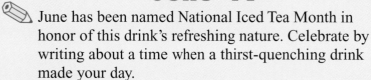
While weeding the garden, you find a stubborn weed that you cannot pull up. Describe what is at the other end of this mysterious weed.

June 18

National Splurge Day is observed in June each year. Celebrate by writing about the one guilty pleasure you would treat yourself to, if only you could.

Garage sales are often held during the summer. What if your mom sold your most prized possession during one such sale? Describe how you would go about finding out who bought it and getting it back.

June 19

The lasagna-loving cartoon strip character Garfield®, created by Jim Davis, first appeared on June 19th, 1978. Write a short letter to Garfield describing several ways in which he could safely lose some weight.

Camping is a popular summer activity. Imagine that while sleeping in a tent, you hear a bear outside. Write about what happens next.

June 20

In honor of Father's Day, celebrated on the third Sunday each June, write about one of the best times you ever had, or would like to have, with your father.

Late one summer night, a neighbor knocks on your door and makes a very strange request. Explain what that request is.

June 21

✏️ Today is the first day of summer in the Northern Hemisphere. If you could add a new season, what would it be like? Name your new season; then describe what kind of weather or new holidays it might have.

✏️ What would happen if you fell asleep in your room one night and woke up somewhere else the next morning? Describe where you woke up and explain what happened.

June 22

✏️ Amateur Radio Week takes place during June. Imagine what life would be like with no television or movies and only the radio for entertainment. Make up a radio show that you might enjoy hearing.

✏️ Having a summer cold is no fun. Write about what you could do to make staying home sick more fun.

June 23

✏️ National Little League Baseball Week begins on the second Monday in June. Do you think there is too much pressure placed on children to excel in sports? Explain.

✏️ Imagine that while flying a kite, a strong gust of wind suddenly picks you up and carries you off to another state before dropping you off. Write about how you get back home.

June 24

✏️ When it is too hot to cook, what do you like to eat? Plan one cool meal for you and your family and describe why it is so refreshing.

✏️ Many graduations take place in June. A common tradition is to throw the graduation cap high into the air at the end of the ceremony. Create a new tradition that might be celebrated when you graduate.

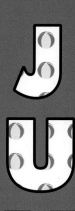

June 25

✐ What would be the perfect summer job for you? Explain a typical day on the job.

✐ After being hired as a student reporter for a sports magazine, you land an exclusive interview with your favorite sports hero! Who is it and what do you learn during the interview?

June 26

✐ Hide-and-seek is a popular summertime game. Describe your favorite hiding place and why you like it so much.

✐ National Forgiveness Day is observed during June. With whom would you most like to smooth things over today? What can you do to make that happen?

June 27

✐ Today is the birth anniversary of Helen Keller. Describe your classroom to someone as if they could not see. Remember to include lots of details to help them imagine what your room "looks" like.

✐ You are playing on the beach when you find several strange-looking footprints in the sand. Your curiosity gets the best of you and you decide to follow the tracks. Describe what happens next.

June 28

✐ National Prevention of Eye Injuries Awareness Week is observed each year in June. Design a new pair of safety goggles with some unique safety features. Now write an advertisement for your goggles that might make someone want to buy them.

✐ Imagine that while working in a laboratory for your summer job, you absentmindedly drink one of the scientist's concoctions. Suddenly you become invisible! Write about what happens next.

June 29

✎ Believe it or not, the Southern Hemisphere is experiencing winter right now! Write a letter to a pen pal there describing your favorite summertime activity.

✎ While trying to clean your room, you hear strange animal sounds coming from your dirty closet. Explain where the sounds are coming from and what happens next.

June 30

✎ Today marks the end of National Burglary Prevention Month. What is your most valuable possession? How would you feel if it was stolen? Write a letter to an imaginary burglar explaining why stealing is wrong.

✎ Imagine that you have temporarily lost your sense of smell. What smell do you miss the most and why?

J U L Y

July 1

On this date in 1847, Congress authorized the first postage stamp. Prior to this, postage was paid by the recipient of the letter, not the sender. Which of the two methods do you think is fairer? Explain your answer.

Today at noon the year is exactly one-half over. Think about the goals you set for yourself back in January. How close are you to achieving those goals? What goals would you still like to accomplish before the year is over?

July 2

Pretend you are a firecracker. Write a story about how you might feel two days before the fourth of July.

The smell of chestnuts roasting, a cold nose, the taste of snowflakes on your tongue. These are some ways that your five senses know it's winter. Write a paragraph describing how your five senses might know it's summer.

July 3

On this date in 1819, the first savings bank in the United States opened in New York. Describe how your life would change if you suddenly became the richest person on earth.

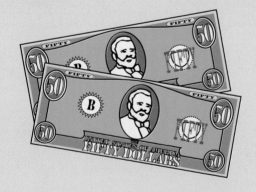

If "April showers bring May flowers," as the old saying goes, what does June bring to July? Try your hand at writing a new saying for these two months.

July 4

Thomas Jefferson, author of the Declaration of Independence, claimed that July 4 was the only birthday he ever celebrated, although he was born on April 13. If you could choose another date on which to celebrate your birthday, what date would you choose and why?

What does the phrase *all-American* mean to you? Write about someone who you feel fits this description.

July 5

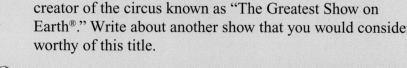 P. T. Barnum was born on this day in 1810. He was the creator of the circus known as "The Greatest Show on Earth®." Write about another show that you would consider worthy of this title.

Pretend you have a pen pal from another country who wants to know about life in the United States. Write your pen pal a letter describing your town.

July 6

Rube Goldberg was an inventor of elaborate machines that performed simple, everyday tasks. Imagine you've invented a machine to perform one of your daily chores. Which chore does it perform? How does your machine work?

July is Anti-Boredom Month. Write about ways you can fight boredom on a day when there's "nothing" to do.

July 7

The first comic book was published on this day in 1802. If you could become any comic book hero, which one would it be and why?

If you knew you were guaranteed success in the next project you attempted, what would you choose to do? Explain your thoughts in a paragraph titled "Sweet Success."

July 8

July is Parenting Month. Write a paragraph describing the kind of parent you would like to be when you grow up.

On this day in 1776, the Declaration of Independence was read in public for the very first time. Describe what life in our country might be like today if it weren't for this revolutionary document.

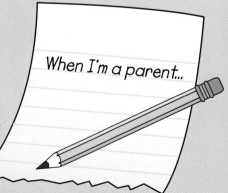

When I'm a parent...

93

July 9

Johnny Weissmuller set a great record on this day in 1922. He became the first to swim 100 meters, freestyle, in less than one minute. To celebrate his achievement, write about a record you would like to break one day.

Think about the sounds you hear before you get out of bed in the morning. Are morning sounds different from evening sounds? Are summer sounds different from winter sounds? Write a paragraph explaining your thoughts.

July 10

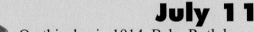

On July 10, 1929, the U.S. government began issuing the paper money we use today. Predict how people will buy goods and services in the year 2029. Write about how you might pay for a vending machine snack, a hamburger, or a toy in the future.

Many people take vacations during the summer. If someone visited your town on vacation, what are some attractions he might see?

July 11

On this day in 1914, Babe Ruth began his career in the major leagues with the Boston Red Sox. His rookie salary that year was $2,900. Today's players make a great deal more than this. Is it reasonable for sports players today to make so much money? Explain your answer.

Imagine you are walking through the woods on a hot summer afternoon. You find a door behind some bushes. When you open it, what do you find?

July 12

July is named after Julius Caesar, who was born on this day in 100 B.C. If you could rename a month after yourself, which month would you choose? What would you call it? Why?

Many stores have "Christmas in July" sales. Write about a memorable shopping trip you had with a parent or friend.

July 13

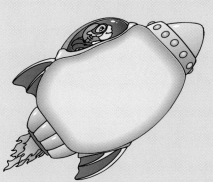

 Advice columnists Ann Landers and Abigail Van Buren were both born in July. Write a letter to an imaginary adviser about a problem you are having. Then answer the letter yourself. What advice can you offer?

 While space travel is currently limited to scientific and military purposes, one day people may be able to travel in space for recreation. Describe the perfect family vacation in space. Where will you go? What will you do while you're there?

July 14

Fighting in the French Revolution began on this day in 1789. In honor of the day freedom was born in France, the French observe July 14 as their Independence Day. Imagine trying to live without the freedoms you have today. Which privileges would you miss the most?

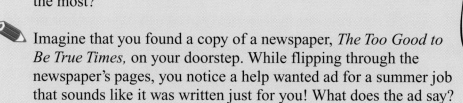 Imagine that you found a copy of a newspaper, *The Too Good to Be True Times,* on your doorstep. While flipping through the newspaper's pages, you notice a help wanted ad for a summer job that sounds like it was written just for you! What does the ad say?

The World's Best Sister

July 15

 Each July, people in Belgium celebrate summer with a walking pageant called *Ommegang,* which means "walk around" in Flemish. Take a mental walk through a real or imaginary place of your choice and describe what you see.

Mother's Day is in mid-May and Father's Day is in mid-June. Pretend today is Siblings Day. What events should take place on this special day to honor brothers and sisters around the world?

July 16

Do you have any cheese?

Apollo 11, the first manned mission to the surface of the Moon, was launched on this date in 1969. List ten items you would pack if you were traveling to the Moon.

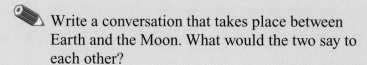 Write a conversation that takes place between Earth and the Moon. What would the two say to each other?

July 17

 Disneyland, "The Happiest Place on Earth," opened its gates on this date in 1955. What is *your* idea of the happiest place on earth? Write a paragraph describing it.

Which are you more like: a kite or a helium balloon? Explain your answer.

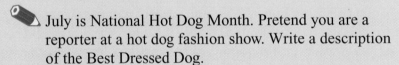

July 18

July is National Ice Cream Month. If you could share an ice-cream cone with anyone in the world, whom would you choose and why?

Describe the taste, texture, and smell of your favorite summertime treat.

July 19

On this date in 1985, George Bell won the "Big Foot" award for his size 28½ foot! Make up an award that only you could win and explain why it is perfect for you and you alone.

July is National Hot Dog Month. Pretend you are a reporter at a hot dog fashion show. Write a description of the Best Dressed Dog.

July 20

Today is the anniversary of the first man to walk on the Moon. Would you like to be an astronaut on the first mission to an unexplored planet or galaxy? Explain your answer.

The first zoo in the United States opened in Philadelphia in July 1874. How do you feel about zoos keeping wild animals on exhibit?

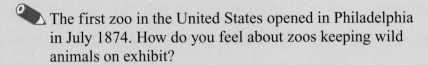

July 21

Write an invitation to a historical event, such as the signing of the Declaration of Independence, as if it were a party. Be sure to include the time, date, place, and purpose of the event. Remind those invited about anything special they need to bring or wear.

Invent a new product for use only in summer. Who should use it? What is it guaranteed to do?

July 22

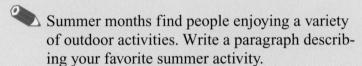
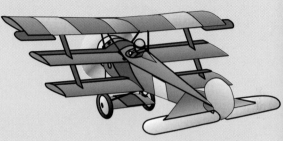

Today is the anniversary of the first solo flight around the world. Write about your first airplane ride. If you have never been on an airplane, describe what you think it would be like.

Summer months find people enjoying a variety of outdoor activities. Write a paragraph describing your favorite summer activity.

July 23

The first swimming school in America opened on this date in 1827, with former president John Quincy Adams as one of the students. When does a person get too old to learn something new? Give reasons for your answer.

A team of scientists is creating a time capsule to send out into space. You have been asked to select two items that would be used to explain summer to someone from another world—a world without seasons. What would you choose to send and why?

July 24

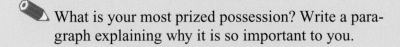

Invent a school of the future—one that you would like to attend. Then write an advertisement which elaborates on the school's best qualities.

What is your most prized possession? Write a paragraph explaining why it is so important to you.

July 25

✏️ Invent a new holiday to be celebrated on this day in July. What occasion does your holiday celebrate? What activities should take place?

✏️ Walter Payton, the Pro Football Hall of Fame running back, was born on this day in 1954. Payton's nickname is "Sweetness." What would your nickname be if you could choose one? If you already have one, what is it and why?

SWEETNESS
10

July 26

✏️ The first sugar cane plantation was started in Hawaii on this date in 1835. Write a paragraph describing the sweetest thing anyone has ever done for you.

✏️ Everybody dreams of the job they will hold in the future. Write about yours.

July 27

✏️ Bugs Bunny made his debut on July 27, 1940. Who is your favorite cartoon character? Explain the reasons for your choice.

✏️ Write a short story that illustrates Thomas Jefferson's observation, "I find that the harder I work, the more luck I seem to have."

July 28

✏️ Today is the birthdate of Beatrix Potter, creator of *The Tale of Peter Rabbit*. Write a paragraph describing your favorite character from a childhood book.

✏️ Imagine that it is so hot outdoors that you can literally fry an egg on the sidewalk! How will you keep cool?

July 29

 On this date in 1900, Louis Lassing of Connecticut created the first hamburger. Pretend today is "Have It Your Way Day." Write about a perfect way to spend the day.

✏️ A distant relative has sent you an airplane ticket to come visit him in a faraway place. When you step off the plane, everything is just like home *except* that nothing is the color it is supposed to be. Describe what you see and explain what has caused this unusual scenery.

July 30

✏️ In 1956, Brenda Lee, an 11-year-old singer from Georgia, recorded her first big hit record. Lee went on to record many more hit songs, a dozen of which made the top ten. What would be the advantages and disadvantages of becoming famous at such a young age?

✏️ A local travel agency is sending you on an all-expense-paid trip to the newly discovered Planet O. Write an advertisement telling potential travelers about your experiences.

July 31

✏️ Henry Perky patented shredded wheat on this date in 1893. Write a radio commercial for a new cereal that will please both nutrition-conscious parents and taste-conscious kids.

✏️ Your school is having a talent show, and every student is required to participate. What talent will you share and why?

Journal

AUGUST

(Student's Name)
Journal

SEPTEMBER

_____

(Student's Name)

Journal

OCTOBER

Journal

NOVEMBER

Journal

DECEMBER

Journal

JANUARY

©1999 The Education Center, Inc. • *730 Journal Prompts* • Intermediate • TEC3171

(Student's Name)

Journal

FEBRUARY

(Student's Name)

Journal

MARCH

(Student's Name)

Journal

APRIL

(Student's Name)

Journal

MAY

(Student's Name)

Journal

JUNE

(Student's Name)

Journal

JULY

Date: _____

_____

_____

_____

_____

_____

_____

_____

_____

_____

_____

_____

_____

_____

_____

_____

_____

_____

_____

_____

_____

_____

_____